More from The Sager Group

The Swamp: Deceit and Corruption in the CIA
An Elizabeth Petrov Thriller (Book 1)
by Jeff Grant

Chains of Nobility: Brotherhood of the Mamluks (Books 1-3)
by Brad Graft

Meeting Mozart: A Novel Drawn from the Secret Diaries of Lorenzo Da Ponte
by Howard Jay Smith

Death Came Swiftly: A Novel About the Tay Bridge Disaster of 1879
by Bill Abrams

A Boy and His Dog in Hell: And Other Stories
by Mike Sager

Eat Wheaties: A Novel
by Michael Kun

Goodbye, Sweetberry Park: A Novel
by Josh Green

Lifeboat No. 8: Surviving the Titanic
by Elizabeth Kaye

Hunting Marlon Brando: A True Story
by Mike Sager

Sing Sing Follies (A Maximum-Security Comedy): And Other True Stories
by John H. Richardson

Who She Was: My Search for My Mother's Life
By Samuel G. Freedman

See our entire library at TheSagerGroup.net_

DISCOVERING MY MOTHER'S SECRET
PAST AS A HOLOCAUST SURVIVOR

Silence Finally Speaks

FRANK FRISTENSKY
WITH PAVEL BAROCH

Silence Finally Speaks: Discovering My Mother's Secret Past as a
Holocaust Survivor

© 2025 Frank Fristensky

Second Edition

Cover art & design, and interior design
by Siori Kitajima, PatternBased.com

Cataloging-in-Publication data for this book
is available from the Library of Congress.

ISBN-13: Second Edition

eBook: 978-1-958861-67-7
Paperback: 978-1-958861-68-4
Hardcover: 978-1-958861-69-1

Published by The Sager Group LLC
(TheSagerGroup.net)

*A first edition was published in the Czech Republic by
Nakladatelství Zed © 2021

DISCOVERING MY MOTHER'S SECRET
PAST AS A HOLOCAUST SURVIVOR

Silence Finally Speaks

FRANK FRISTENSKY
WITH PAVEL BAROCH

THE SAGER GROUP

Artifex Te Adiuva

Dedication

To my children, Hana, Misha, Nadia, their descendants, to all relatives of the Klein, Aschermann, Fristensky families, and to all the victims of the Holocaust. Thank you also to everyone who contributed to the creation of this book.

Contents

Foreword

Dear Readers,

If you allow me, I will hold you up for a little while before you begin reading the first chapter of this book that I wholeheartedly recommend. Because I am ahead of you: I read it when it was still a manuscript, but, more importantly, I also know the life story of the book's heroine. I belong to the family that took in the orphaned Hana Kleinova after the war.

For the girl who survived internment in the Terezin Ghetto (in then Czechoslovakia), the suffering did not end. Doomed entries were added to her fate. The eldest of her three sons began to uncover his mother's life story from the pre-war and post-war years for himself when he could not personally witness it. He did not know anything about it. Like many others, his mother did not want to burden her offspring with a past that was so painful for her and the whole family.

Frank (Frantisek) Fristensky was very successful in his search. He was fortunate that he could still interview for testimony from those who, like his mother, had lived through the suffering of the Terezin Ghetto and survived. Yet part of Hana Kleinova's life story remains shrouded in mystery. Witnesses are already absent. And most importantly, the son could not ask the one from whom he would have learned the most—his mother. But, as Frank bitterly notes, his mother would probably not have told him anything about her internment in the Terezin Ghetto. In the post-Soviet period, when Aunt Hanka, as we called her at home, began to return to her homeland from Switzerland, when she finally returned for good, I used to meet her often. She no longer pushed past experiences away. When she arrived in Zabreh na Morave, she asked me to take her to the church of the Czech Brotherhood congregation where she was getting married. I also accompanied her to the New Jewish Cemetery in Prague to the grave of her grandmother and her grandfather. There was a lot that she told me about, that she shared with me. But she never talked about her Terezin Ghetto experience.

It is good that author Frank Fristensky and Czech editor Pavel Baroch have together written this book about Hana Kleinova. We should not forget what painful experiences many of our fellow citizens had to go through. Pavel Baroch has previously recorded and written the dramatic fate of the Jewish boy Jiri Fiser, who, together with his twin brother Josef, survived Auschwitz at the age of eight, including the pseudo-scientific experiments of Josef Mengele.

There are several Jewish heroines in our literature with a moving life story. Ivan Olbracht, the author of the novel *O smutných očích Hany Karadžičové* (*The Sad Eyes of Hana Karadzicova*), did not let the heroine know about the hell of the concentration camps because he concluded his story before the Holocaust. But it is quite possible that the real Hana did not escape the cruel reality. And Dita Saxova, the heroine of the novel of the same name by Arnost Lustig, the well-known author with whom Hana Kleinova later became friends, tries in vain to break free from the oppression of the past. Both literary novels have been made into movies. It is quite possible that this book, too, will catch the attention of a movie-maker.

In the meantime, let's look forward to the fact that Frank Fristensky and Pavel Baroch are going to tell the dramatic life story of Frank's grandfather, Frantisek Fristensky who, like his brother Gustav, was an accomplished athlete-wrestler, although not as famous as Gustav, in book form. Grandson Frank decided to reveal the fate of his father's family ancestors.

—Pavel Taussig, PhD*

*Publicist, author, professor, Czech movie historian, screenplay writer of the movie *Kolja*, Golden Globe Award winner for Best Foreign Language Film

Notes on the Translation of this book from Czech to English

This story has been translated from Czech to English and has undergone many revisions with an American reader in mind. For those educated in the US school systems, the standard history curricula, unfortunately, do not include much, if any, on Czechoslovakia's history and its role in WWII. The notorious Auschwitz, Bergen-Belsen, Dachau, and other concentration camps are identifiable in typical school textbook readings, but personally I had never heard of the Terezin Ghetto (in what was then Czechoslovakia) before working on this project. And like the history, many of the Czech geographical locations are also unfamiliar. However, Frank does a remarkable job leading the reader through the dark corridors with detailed explanation and helpful "Historical Stops" throughout, in tandem with the narrative, leaving the door open to more investigation and research for the curious and interested.

The structure of this story is unique in that it is an interlocking frame story which begins with the author's recollection of the day he was told of his mother's death. From there it retraces earlier days when he wondered about the mystery of his mother's past. Hana's personal story is then told within this outline. However, the author's voice frequently "steps in" to provide context and sourcing to lend credibility and support. This approach also reveals the overlap of his own story and its role in the historical landscape. The story comes full-circle with the legacy of Hana and her grandchildren.

Efforts have been made to maintain the integrity of the original names and places for smoother reading. Major cities and locations are anglicized and tend to drop any pronunciation accent and other marks that are prominent in the Czech language. Another consideration is how names are culturally used, particularly for women. For example, the protocol for women's surnames utilize -ova as a feminine suffix. The last name "Klein" becomes "Kleinova." If a woman is married, the name becomes hyphenated with a feminine suffix also added to her husband's surname: "Kleinova-Fristenska." The English equivalent is Klein Fristensky. This occurs frequently when referencing interviews of women and others who knew Fristensky's mother. The full married names of women are used even when referencing them as girls in Terezin because so much of the narrative includes direct quotes from these women as adults.

Fristensky has conducted countless interviews and extensive research for this work, which itself was a challenging feat given the small window of time he had to locate many of the people who knew his mother because over fifty years had passed by the time he could reach out to them. To call the work pure nonfiction though would be something of a misnomer. There is a challenge in confirming the details of conversations or some specific personal events given Hana never shared all of her story firsthand. However, Hana Klein Fristensky's life leading up to her time in Terezin and the years that followed have been carefully pieced together and recreated in this narrative as close as possible to how her life unfolded. The conditions, sequence of the events, and people involved are all fact-based on much research and many interviews.

The foremost intent was to tell a vivid true story amidst the chronicle of Terezin's Holocaust history. There is still so much more to tell, and I wanted to know so much more, with questions about the victims and historical stances, but the focus is narrowed here to Hana's story. Just the idea that an account can generate motivation to discover more is a "win" for any writer, particularly one who is revealing the truths of the Holocaust and the legacy of its victims.

—R. White, translation editor

Introduction: Never Again

At the end of September 1968, the sports hall in Vienna (Wiener Stadthalle) was full of refugees from Czechoslovakia. They were fleeing from the Soviets' and their Allies' tanks that had occupied their country the month before. When Hana Kleinova-Fristenska walked through the corridor to the rim of the huge sports arena with her husband Jaromir and three sons (Frank, Jarek, and Zbynek), she stopped for a moment and looked around. There was head after head; people were either sitting on the bleachers or lying down between them with their few belongings shambolically spread around. Dirt and stench. Hana's face looked sad, eyes and mouth wide open. Suddenly a twenty-five-year-old memory sprang forth in Hana's mind. "I never want to experience a concentration camp again," she sobbed. It was the first and last time I heard my mother mention her cruel youth experience. I didn't know the meaning of it. And it was the first time I saw tears on her face.

As I found out much later, my mother, when not yet fourteen years of age, spent three years (1942-1945) in the Jewish ghetto of Terezin. Her mother, Marta Kleinova, saved her from being transported to the Auschwitz killing camp. She managed to forge documents and board a cattle truck in her daughter's place. It was the sacrifice of a lifetime. Marta was murdered on a death march toward the East from Auschwitz in one of the winter months of 1945. Her husband, Rudolf Klein, ended up in the gas chamber upon arriving at Auschwitz on October 18, 1944. Hana's brother, Petr, who was three years older, survived Auschwitz and another forced labor camp in Germany.

However, I did not find out the details of my mother's fate until many decades later. When she died in 1998, I began to search for her past, which she had never spoken about. I sought answers to so many questions about those significant parts of her life that were never shared. Was she trying to erase the horrifying memories of three years in hell? Was it to protect her children, whom she never intended to have after returning from Terezin? And what did she think when, after the Nazi occupation in the spring of 1939 and the introduction of anti-Semitic laws, her friends at school suddenly called to her, "You dirty Jew!" What was going through her mind as she entered the gates of the Terezin Ghetto at the age of fourteen? What did she say to her favorite doll she was carrying with her from home? How did she experience the difficult period in the life of every young girl in Terezin, as she transformed from a child into a woman? How did she cope with the first love of her life, which she also experienced in the cruel environment of the ghetto? After liberation, how did she cope with the fact that a significant part of her family did not survive the Holocaust, including her parents, grandparents, and over seventy members of her family? Did she blame herself that she survived, and her mother, father, and other relatives did not?

In 1978, I moved from Switzerland to the United States and changed my first name Frantisek to Frank. But it wasn't until many years after my mother's death that I began to do research in the archives, collecting pertinent documents and memories of my mother and her ancestors from both my grandfather's and grandmother's families, the Kleins and the Aschermanns. I also talked to her fellow prisoners from Terezin. From one of them, seventy-two years later, I learned a seventy-two-year-old secret . . . the biggest secret my mother never told anyone during her lifetime. As a young prisoner, she experienced her first love, however, with a tragic conclusion.

I was very fortunate to have been able to meet other survivors, then her age. Some never knew Hana, some remembered her from the vegetable gardens where most of them worked, and, most impressively, some ladies remembered her very well because they shared the same room—Room 29. I also found several places where Hana and her family lived in Prague before being transported to Terezin. I researched the fate of the Fristensky family, made so famous by the well-known wrestler Gustav Fristensky. At times, my search resembled the mazes of a complex detective work. It took great effort. By then, I was determined to learn as much as I could about my mother.

I resolved that I must pass on what I would find out to my children, to my other family members, and to other people who understand what it means to learn from history.

Many times, I couldn't even believe what I was learning, even things beyond the Terezin Ghetto. I found out that my mother's Jewish curse didn't end with the fall of the Third Reich. Even in peacetime, it became clear how deeply rooted anti-Semitism was in certain social levels.

My long pursuit of my mother Hana's past has brought me ever closer to her. She has been gone from this world for more than twenty-five years, but I am closer to her and understand her much more deeply than when she was alive. I talk to her, and she guides me through her "unknown" life for me. I am in a hurry, afraid that she will go away again, and I am not going to be able to hear or write anything about her again. I told myself that if I wanted to know as much as possible about myself, and indeed about my children, I had to know my parents, in this case my mother. I know she is telling me to record her life story for those who will come after me. She was not able to write it down. She couldn't even talk about it. It was too painful for her.

—Frank Fristensky
March 2025

Chapter 1

The Phone Rings

On the last day of July 1998 in Durango, Colorado, the phone rang in my house. In the very early morning hours, the hands on the clock showed 3:00 a.m. My sleep had never been very deep, so I could hear the insistent sharp jangling of the phone clearly. My heart raced a little. Who would call at such an ungodly hour? A phone call in the middle of the night rarely delivers good news. But maybe it was just a mistake, just a wrong number.

My wife, Victoria, was the first one out of bed. With a sleepy shuffling step, she headed to the kitchen to answer the phone. In a few seconds, she was completely awake; the events that followed seemed more like a bad dream.

"No, that's not possible," my wife screamed into the phone. She turned toward the bedroom and called out to me. I was half-asleep, but my brain was sensing a distressing message was coming. I quickly got out of bed and ran to the phone as several of the darkest scenarios of what could have happened ran through my head.

On the other end of the line was my younger brother Jarek. He was calling from Chur, a town in Switzerland where he and my mother lived. "Muti [mother] has died," he said in a seemingly calm voice. He told me that neighbors had found her in her apartment.

I was in shock, my heart in rapid palpitations, my throat tightening. But I still managed to tell my brother I would call him later. After the news, I couldn't vocalize anything further. I fell to the ground, my eyes filled with tears, overcome with a feeling of shock and disbelief over what I had just heard. Victoria was sobbing, bent over on the kitchen counter. I don't even know how long I remained collapsed on the floor. When I regained my composure, I called Jarek back.

But my thoughts reverted back to the previous day, when my mother was still alive, and I was on a regular weekly phone call with her. She sounded so happy. She was still full of strength and vigor, and as a woman of seventy years old, she had not suffered from any serious illness.

"I just got home from town," she had shared in the weekly call. "It was a beautiful day, but hot and humid in Roznov [a town in the

Czech Republic]. I had coffee and a nice chat with my friends Blanka and Dana." Then, just a few hours later, she is dead.

There was so much I had yet to learn about her.

I suspected my mother, Hana, had secrets, but she took many of them to her grave: memories of three years of her life during the Holocaust in the Jewish ghetto in Terezin (Theresienstadt in German) and of her parents, older brother, and extended family. She never spoke about them with me or my two siblings. Hers was a buried past. Over the years, I had a gut feeling there was more to her life story, from various clues and hints suggested by relatives about this lost period of her life. However, none of it was confirmed until after her passing. Not long before she died, I cautiously asked her about her parents and if she was a Jew. She had always shrugged such questions off, and this instance was no different.

I asked her, "You're Jewish. Your parents were Jewish too. What happened to them? Why don't I have a second grandmother and grandfather like other people?"

There were always the familiar brush-off answers: "I'll tell you later" or "Now is not a good time." She once said of her parents (my grandfather and grandmother), "They both died shortly before the war." I didn't get any specific answers—about life for her in the ghetto, about the fact that my grandparents were transported to Auschwitz, where they were killed. To this day, I often wonder if I should have pressed her more, forced her to tell me. But I always felt there was more time and that she would eventually decide to share these things with me. How could I have known that she would die such an unexpected and sudden death at only seventy years old? She should have had more time.

My journey to Terezin would be a profound and enduring one. Since the early revelations of my mother's past, I have read many books written mostly by Terezin survivors, including life stories from the Holocaust and countless articles. I have also seen documentaries and visited museums and archives in Prague. I have been to Terezin, Beit Theresienstadt in Givat Haim-Ihud, Israel, and Auschwitz and have read interviews with concentration camp survivors and their children and other relatives. I interviewed over twenty Terezin survivors, most of whom were Hana's roommates in Terezin, or those who worked with her in the gardening and agricultural aspects of the camp, and I even spoke to those who just knew of her. Throughout all of this research, I learned that there are two basic groups of Holocaust survivors.

The first group does not hide their fate in their hearts. They confide their personal experiences, their suffering, to the outside world. It is a way for them to cope with the death of their loved ones who were not so fortunate and did not live to see the end of the war. Many of them have become public advocates of historical knowledge of the Holocaust and defenders of human rights, diverse religious beliefs, and tolerance. They strive to ensure that the generations that come after them will never forget. Often, they have retraced the steps of their friends and acquaintances to remember together their time in the ghettos or concentration camps. In such moments, they sought relief for their scarred souls. This first group includes, for example, the writer Arnost Lustig, a friend of our family, who also knew the hell of the Terezin Ghetto, as well as that of the Auschwitz extermination camp. He dedicated a substantial part of his work to the topic of the Holocaust.

My mother Hana, however, belonged to the second group of survivors, the silent, secretive ones. They kept all their experiences, suffering, feelings, emotions, and memories to themselves. Never giving a voice to the horrors of the past was their way of dealing with it. Silent.

The following is the life story of my mother, Hana Kleinova-Fristenska—a special woman about whom, I much later discovered, I knew her present without knowing her past—I have researched and documented it as close to her life events as possible, filling the gaps of her story based on the context of what I have learned and what I can only surmise.

Chapter 2

Lustig's Idea

The early autumn of 1978 was hot and humid in Washington, DC. Anyone who went outside was sweating within minutes. Still, I often and very happily made the trek on foot to Arnost Lustig's home from my house on Keokuk Street, which stood exactly on the border between the District of Columbia and the state of Maryland. I knew very well what was in store for me that evening. Even as I entered the several-story apartment building on Tunlaw Street, the pleasant aroma of what was cooking in Arnost Lustig's family home could be smelled downstairs at the reception desk. Even the doorman was smiling, because I always told him what would be for dinner—he had undoubtedly never eaten roast duck with cabbage and dumplings.

Lustig's apartment, where he lived with his wife Vera, son Josef, and daughter Eva, always looked like some kind of archive. The walls were covered with family photos, paintings by various Czech artists, and Czech cartoons clipped from newspapers, which Arnost liked very much. The aroma of duck was enhanced by Czech songs emanating from the record player. His study was littered with books, papers, all sorts of files, nondescript figurines, and everything that perhaps inspired his creativity. And in the midst of all this, there was Arnost, wearing only a T-shirt and shorts, always in a good mood and smiling—perhaps in part because he knew what would be on his dinner plate.

He leaned over his typewriter, pounding on the keyboard with two fingers so fast that his index fingers were a blur. The woodpecker-like hammering of keys hitting paper echoed through the study. It was a sight to behold. The clatter died down as he lifted his head and turned to me. "Would you like to write a story about your mother too? I'll help you with that if you want," he offered. Perhaps he assumed I knew more of my mother's history than I actually did.

My mother never talked about her past, at least not in my presence. I didn't know there was a story worth telling. I was focused on my own life going forward, not looking backward at someone else's life. I was not yet thirty years old and needed to get settled in the United States after my second "emigration," this time from

Switzerland. The first emigration took place when I fled my home-land of Czechoslovakia a decade earlier.

Arnost Lustig, and his family too, fled from Soviet tanks after August 21, 1968. Before the Soviet invasion, Arnost was in former Yugoslavia, working on a script for a movie about General Tito. Our family had met the Lustigs through a great coincidence, but fate would probably have brought us together anyway. His wife, Vera, and daughter Eva were driving to Switzerland to visit Eva's brother Pepi in Zurich when their car broke down. It was not far from where another Czech emigrant family lived—the Fristensky family. Passers-by directed Mrs. Lustig to her compatriots, i.e., to us. Our families became friends.

In 1970, the Lustigs moved to the United States. Arnost was a respected writer and journalist. After I arrived in the US, he gave me temporary asylum in his apartment. With his help, I got a position at American University in Washington, DC, where he was a professor of literature. I became a physical education teacher and a coach of the university's women's volleyball team.

His suggestion to write my mother's story fell on deaf ears that night. At that moment, I was more interested in the delicious roasted duck that Vera was preparing for dinner. Even so, Arnost had put a bug in my head.

From that day on, during my frequent visits to the Lustig home, I unwittingly began to learn about the Holocaust. In fact, I heard for the first time that my mother had spent her young years in the Terezin Ghetto—as had Arnost Lustig, although they did not meet for the first time until after the war. At that time, I was not even aware of what Terezin was about and had little interest; even Judaism escaped my understanding. I was not raised as a Jew. My focus was only on my dream job of coaching. However, those early visits and conversations with Arnost did plant the seeds of curiosity for what I would uncover years later about my mother, and in turn, about myself.

<u>The First Historical Stop</u>

The Third Wave of Emigration

The mass emigration after August 21, 1968, was the third to hit Czechoslovakia in the 20th century. The first wave came in 1938 and 1939, first after the Munich Agreement and then after the establishment of the Protectorate of Bohemia and Moravia. The second followed the rise of the communist dictatorship in February 1948. The third followed the Soviet occupation in August 1968. By 1969, more than 100,000 people had left Czechoslovakia, many of them to Austria, while other countries of exile were Germany, Switzerland, Great Britain, and also the United States and Canada. Important personalities left the country, including writers, actors, architects, engineers, and other intellectuals.

For example, a report by the State Security Service in Pilsen, from the turn of 1968 and 1969, describes this: "As of January 1, 1969, 590 adults and 249 children had been found to be illegally emigrating within the West Bohemian Region. Compared to the previous year, when on the same date the number of adults and children abroad without permission was 227 and 47 respectively, the number of children is disproportionately higher this year."

The report noted that most of the people escaping from Czechoslovakia believed they could find better living conditions and employment elsewhere:

> This is evidenced by the increase in emigration after August 21, 1968, when a large number of people became convinced that as a result of the events of August, the political situation in our country would change and that living conditions, including the standard of living, would not improve in the foreseeable future. In isolated cases, especially among those who emigrated just after August 21, 1968, there was also a fear of reprisals for their involvement in the post-January period in 1968. A larger number of people, in addition to looking for a better existence abroad, also dealt with personal problems such as disagreements in their marriages, workplaces, etc. For another, not particularly large group, the decisions were motivated by the nature and character of the adventurous persons. These are essentially the main motives for emigration, apart from a few specific reasons.

In its report, the Pilsen State Police also pointed out an increase in the number of emigrants with university education, from eleven in 1967 to eighty-four in

1968. The communist security forces had already begun to close the passages to the West in 1969, making immigration more difficult. Even so, many people were trying to get out of the wiretapped Czechoslovakia and into the free world. Some lost their lives trying to cross the Iron Curtain. According to the Institute for the Study of Totalitarian Regimes, 270 names are recorded from 1948 to 1989. The exact number is not known because the communist authorities kept some cases of "trespassers" secret.

Although I allowed our friend's idea of writing my mother's life story to go in one ear and out the other, Hana Kleinova's fate still nagged me—it was the most unabating for me years later as my life took me to many places. I lived in the US until 1988, then moved my family to Switzerland until 1996. We returned to the US to settle in Durango, CO, before ultimately moving back to the Czech Republic permanently in 2018. By this time, Czechoslovakia had become two distinct countries: the Czech Republic and Slovakia. However, I had already started returning to my home country earlier. The first time was not long after November 1989. And then more and more often.

In 2003, I set up a personal travel agency in Durango—quite amateurishly. I traveled with small groups of Americans almost every year to the Czech Republic and other Central European countries. Along the way, I told my life story, showing the places where I had faced Soviet tanks as a demonstrator on Wenceslas Square in August 1968 and described my subsequent emigration. Many times, I also talked about the athletic Fristensky family, about my grandfather Frantisek and his more famous brother Gustav. I also talked about what my mother and her whole family had experienced during the Holocaust—about which, at that point, I still knew very little.

My stories were very well received, and more and more of my American friends urged me to write my life story, even telling me that it could easily be a Hollywood blockbuster. Eventually, I was convinced and started writing the part I knew personally and therefore best: the escape from communism, life in the West, and my discovery of America. The more often I reflected, the broader the story became. But then there was a major hitch. I had mapped out the Fristensky family thoroughly, but when it came to my mother, I found that I knew almost nothing about her. I mean, at least until I was old enough to be aware of the world around me. Her life before 1948, before I was born, was a great mystery to me. I must confess this revelation took me quite by surprise. My story then seemed to switch gears; my focus redirected. I didn't want to write about myself anymore; I wanted to write about my mother, her family, about what she experienced during the occupation. I wanted to write her story that was never told. The bug that Arnost Lustig had planted in my head years earlier had finally awakened.

I began to search for all available material about the Holocaust and WWII—books, articles, memoirs, interviews of survivors, and much more. In my family archives, I also found many pre-war photographs of my parents, and my grandmother and grandfather alongside my mother, little "Hanka," as she was affectionately called by family and friends. But I kept running into my mother's silence. And sometimes I even discovered that my children knew more about her than I did, simply because my mother occasionally and randomly told her grandchildren something of her childhood. One such discovery was when I found out that my great-grandmother taught my mother a poem that she had composed herself: "I am a little girl—they call me Hanicka. They put me in a purse—and drive me up the ass" (It rhymes well in Czech). And I remember, while living in Roznov pod Radhostem (Roznov for short), there was a huge brown hard leather travel bag that was always stored in one of our closets and was never used for anything. As little kids, we played with it, putting my youngest brother (Zbynek) in it and swinging him around. Around that time, my mother told me the poem's history. It was the first time she ever mentioned her grandmother to me.

But I couldn't convince my mother to discuss her past in any depth.

In the wake of her passing, those seeds of curiosity were growing. After 1998 I started going to the Czech Republic more frequently, and I was meeting quite often with Pavel Taussig (a family friend who knew much about my mother). But the real catalyst for my journey was sparked by Pavel's mother Alenka, who provided an amazing interview in 2004. From that point forward, it was slowly but steadily making some sense to me about my mother's past.

The Girls of Room 28, a book I came across while looking for authentic documents, proved to be the key to uncovering her story. In it, author Hannelore Brenner-Wonschick chronicled the fate of several girls from Terezin Ghetto. My mother Hana lived in the same barrack in Terezin, on the same floor, and even next door—in Room 29. The real breakthrough for me came in 2015 when I contacted Brenner-Wonschick in Berlin.

Then it snowballed.

I wrote to the author, and did not have to wait long for Hannelore's reply. It came almost immediately. And in it were contacts of other women who had survived Terezin. I later met them in the United States, Israel, and the Czech Republic. They told me their stories, which I recorded. And, in turn, they put me in touch with other women, other survivors. The stories multiplied. It turned out that Hana's friends from the ghetto were also among these women. The timing of my meetings with them was fortunate. They were nearly ninety years old. However, some who knew my mother had died, and I was too late to meet them.

Without this fleeting sliver of time with these women, the stories would be forever unknown to me.

Chapter 3

Testimony of Family Photos

One summer day in 1991, I was returning to Chur from Prague with my mother and my three children. We had visited relatives there. We were just passing through the Smichov section of Prague when I asked my mother, "Is this somewhere where you lived before the war?" My mother threw a quick surprising glance at me, as if she was wondering where I might have learned this. I didn't tell her that my cousin had told me, even though she didn't know the exact address either. I gripped the steering wheel tighter and tried again, "But it was around here, wasn't it?" No response. "Probably somewhere up there on the hill," I directed with a pointed tilting nod of my head. "Or don't you remember?" Nothing; silence; silence.

The impenetrable wall my mother established stood firm, and it was not until years later, after her death, that I had to start my own search for my mother's birthplace in Prague.

In a family album from the pre-war years, there are many photographs of a cute little girl with short-cropped dark hair. She's smiling. She appears full of joy, just like her parents and other relatives. That little girl is my mother, Hana. She was born on June 21, 1928, in Prague, the second child of Rudolf and Marta Klein, who had been living on Jagellonska Street for several years. Hana's brother Petr was three years older, born in September 1925. When Hana was two years old, the family moved to a larger apartment that Rudolf's father had rented on Na Vrsku Street in Prague-Smichov. But even there, the Kleins did not stay long; they wanted a house of their own and looked for it again in Smichov. This part of Prague must have been very dear to the hearts of my grandparents. After a long search, the Kleins bought a villa with a garden on Na Provaznici Street in Smichov.

The villa at this address, which I have visited many times since my mother's death, is still standing today. It is a large, several-story, light building surrounded by mature trees in the adjacent garden. It was here that a young Hana often played with her brother Petr and her cousin Ivan, who was the same age as she was. Right below the Kleins' house was the home of her father's sister Anna and her family. This was still a carefree life for the children; no one minded their Jewish origin. Often after school, Hana went to a small nearby park to play with her cousin Ivan.

I managed to find a purchase contract dated November 17, 1932, according to which the purchase price was agreed at CZK 350,000. The price of the villa shows that the Kleins did not live modestly at all. Quite the contrary. And it seemed likely the Great Depression did not have any significant impact on their standard of living. Hana's father worked as a *procures* (director of sales) for the Julius Kussi company based in Prague. The company distributed pharmaceutical and chemical goods all over Europe. I managed to find an important related document with basic information about my grandfather. It is a passport application by Rudolf Klein from 1921. The purpose of the trips, he wrote, was for the sale of pharmaceutical and chemical goods. He intended to visit Austria, Poland, Germany, Bulgaria, Romania, and Greece.

"There is no objection to the issuance of a passport," wrote an employee of the police headquarters in Prague. Rudolf traveled abroad quite often. He did not talk much about his work with his family, but he was undoubtedly very successful. He was the right-hand man to the company owner, Mr. Kussi, who empowered him to do many things, effectively making him general manager with quite a wide range of power.

My grandfather, Rudolf, was born in the village of Oselce, about an hour's drive southwest of Pilsen. Rudolf Klein and his family often traveled from Prague to visit his home village, as evidenced by the photos in the family album. "I loved my grandmother because she always had time for us children and gave us all kinds of goodies. She cooked very well," my mother revealed years later in a rare bit of commentary from her childhood memories. And then she added, "Sometimes she would take us kids aside so no one could hear us, and she would tell us rude jokes."

While Hana's father worked hard to substantially support the family, her mother was a homemaker. She had two helpers on hand—a nanny and a cook—further evidence that the family was quite wealthy. On weekends and other free days, the whole family was together. Rudolf owned a car, so they drove around the

Bohemian and Moravian countryside and also visited other relatives. As witnessed through many surviving pictures from their outings in the 1930s, it must have been among their favorite free-time activities. Some of the photographs show as many as ten people. Under one black and white picture, it is written, "Aunt Blanka, Hrensko mountain 1937." I have not been able to find out who all the people in the photos are, but I assume that they are more distant relatives or family friends.

Aunt Marie Aschermannova, who was called Mancina, used to be their frequent companion on trips. The children liked her very much. She was a kind of unofficial nanny. Her father was Arthur Aschermann, a well-known physician from Prague. He was friends with the renowned Czech sportscaster and journalist Josef Laufer and members of the famous Czech soccer club of Slavia Prague.

When the family was at home in Smichov, Hana spent much of her free time with children from the surrounding area. Since she took piano lessons, she often practiced at home in the evenings. Her father bought the piano after the family had moved to the villa in Smichov. She also learned English. My grandfather, Rudolf, was fond of Old Master paintings and porcelain antiques, which were scattered all over the house. My grandmother, on the other hand, liked to read books, especially by Czech authors, and she and her husband often went to the theater and opera at the National, Svandovo, or Vinohrady theaters. I once learned from Marie Aschermannova that my grandmother Marta was a friend of Olga Scheinpflugova, the wife of a well-known Czech author, Karel Capek. I remember our home had several books by Capek, which were personally autographed by him.

In the mid-1930s, Hana Kleinova started primary school. But which one? I contacted several authorities in Prague, but none of them could answer me. The Prague City Archives wrote to me that they had also found no record of my mother, but that she had probably attended the fourth or fifth grade of the municipal girls' school in Smichov in U Santosky Street, or Graficka Street. "These two schools (especially the fourth general girls' school in Prague XVI) would be the most likely, given the residence of the Klein family, and the reported residences of the other pupils confirm this assumption," an archivist wrote to me.

Later, I discovered my mother had contacted several institutions and organizations, after our move to Switzerland in 1968, seeking information regarding her past. There was a letter that surfaced from the 1970s, where she wrote to an office: "From 1934 to 1939, I went to primary school in Prague and then for six months to a second-grade English school. Because of the anti-Jewish laws, the schools were then closed to us, and I was no longer able to complete my education." The elementary school in U Santosky Street was indeed not far from the family home. Perhaps her father took her by car some mornings, but I suppose she usually walked with her brother Petr and cousin Ivan. It was downhill, and the trip could be made in twenty minutes. It was more challenging on the way home, with a long uphill hike for the children.

Very soon the first major turning point in their lives would occur: the German occupation.

Chapter 4

The Beginning of Evil

It was the transition from September to October 1938.

There are no existing journals that Hana possibly wrote during that time, nor have any letters emerged showing that her parents might have written anything describing the events of the period. But there are enough stories from their peers to help in imagining what that time was like for them.

Hana noticed her mother sitting at the kitchen table, looking very worried. Hana didn't really comprehend; she was only ten years old, and there was no clear understanding of the news that was infiltrating the adult world. She had no idea that her mother was distressed because the Republic had suddenly lost a third of its territory following the Munich Agreement of September 30, 1938, a settlement reached by Germany, Great Britain, France, and Italy (without any Czechoslovakian representation) that permitted German annexation of the Sudetenland, in the border regions of northern and western Bohemia and northern Moravia. The Krkonose Mountains, where the Klein family loved to vacation during both summer and winter seasons, had also been absorbed by the German Reich.

Hana's father, Rudolf, gently stroked his wife's hair to dispel her anxiety and tried to reassure her that everything would be fine, that she had nothing to worry about. At this time, nobody could possibly anticipate that it would get worse. Much worse. In the months and years that followed, Rudolf would have to resort to similar gestures and reassurances more and more often as the position of the Jewish population in the country was steadily deteriorating.

Anti-Semitic sentiments were growing in the still-free Second Czechoslovakian Republic, composed of Bohemia, Moravia, Silesia, and the autonomous regions of Slovakia and the Subcarpathian Rus. The Second Czechoslovakian Republic was the political system from October 1, 1938 to March 15, 1939 as a result of the 1938 Munich agreement. It would be dissolved when the Germans invaded it on March 15, 1939. Increasing anti-Semitism could not have left the Klein parents with much comfort. Most likely, though, they tried to maintain a calm atmosphere within the family in the Smichov villa—to protect and insulate their children as much as possible.

Today, I can no longer ask them how they felt as Jews, what they experienced every day, or how they perceived the future. But I am convinced that they were clearly aware of the impending evil, even though they could not conceive of its enormity. Who would have imagined at the time that systematic killing of the Jewish population would claim a staggering six million victims?

It is important to note that the majority of society of the pre-war Czech lands had no fundamental problem with the Jewish community, as evidenced, among other things, by the number of Jewish-Christian marriages. In Bohemia, such marriages accounted for nearly forty-four percent of unions. In Moravia, it was thirty percent.

The Second Historical Stop

One Thousand Years of Jews in the Czech Lands

The earliest surviving written sources confirm the presence of Jewish merchants in Prague as early as the tenth century. Historians also place the beginning of the settlement of Jews in the Czech lands in the same century. Jewish merchants settled mainly around European trade routes or in important settlements such as Prague, Brno, Olomouc, or Znojmo.

The first Jewish settlements are known from the eleventh century in the Prague suburbs and around Vysehrad. They disappeared after the Jewish population moved to a new settlement on the right bank of the Vltava River (today's Josefov Quarter), which became their center and remained so for many centuries. "Until the beginning of the thirteenth century, they were considered almost foreigners, they traded freely natural products and finished goods, they were apparently free to choose where to live, they could practice crafts, acquire land and houses. Some of them worked at courthouses as high court officials," wrote Tomas Pekny in his book History of the Jews in Bohemia and Moravia.

One interesting discovery from this period was made during extensive archaeological research between 2004 and 2005 at the site where the Palladium department store now stands on Namesti Republiky (Republic Square) in the center of Prague. There, archaeologists found a gold ring, weighing 0.35 ounces, with a dark green oval stone and an inscription in Hebrew. The letters MSH BR SLMH stand for "Moshe bar Shlomo" (Moses' son of Solomon), who was probably the owner of the item, who may have lost it here.

Initially, the Jewish population was viewed as Zionist, so no restrictive measures were applied against them.

> *Later, with the growing authority of Christianity and its representatives, anti-Jewish attitudes began to assert themselves in Christian theology, which gradually influenced the factual position of Jews in society . . . For medieval man, religion was the most important principle of life, a complete worldview, an anchor in society, and his own identity. Any deviation from the boundaries of the doctrine in which he was brought up meant exclusion from family, society, and even his own life and damnation. To understand that someone held different values and ideas was unacceptable to a medieval man. It follows that harmonious coexistence between Christians and Jews was impossible in the medieval world. Jews were seen as a symbol of Evil and the Devil on Earth, as the killers of the Christian God. (Holocaust.cz)*

The position of Jews in European countries, including those of Bohemia, gradually changed. They were considered inferior people and had to live in separate quarters—ghettos. If they wanted to leave the ghetto, they had to wear a visible marking, for example an armband, a circle on their coat, and, in Prague, a special hat. Jews were not allowed to own land or make a living outside the ghetto. Holocaust.cz stated, "money trading and lending at interest became a reserved activity for Jews, which was marked as undesirable and unclean for Christians. Jewish financiers, however, were widely used by other people, as [did] the rulers, who borrowed large sums of money from the Jews." It is likely this activity spawned anti-Semitic character attacks on Jews for usury that still exist today.

Some anti-Semitic prejudices also come from the Middle Ages, such as one about Jews poisoning wells with the plague and murdering Christian virgins and children for their ritual purposes. A specific historical example centered on the Jew Leopold Hilsner. He was accused, based on only circumstantial evidence, of the ritual murder of nineteen-year-old Anezka Hruzova near Polna in the Highlands at the end of the nineteenth century, and he spent nineteen years in prison before he was pardoned. Tomas Garrigue Masaryk (first Czech President 1918-1937) intervened significantly in the events of the time, describing the ritual murder as superstition and considering the background to the trial as anti-Semitic, which earned him the hatred of a large part of the public.

"It was a bad campaign, the 'Hilsner-raid', when I had to fight the superstition of ritual murder," Masaryk later confided to the writer Karel Capek. "I was not interested in the Hilsner trial at first, but a former pupil of mine from Vienna, the writer Sigismund Munz, a Moravian, came to see me, and he made me come forward. I knew about ritual superstition from the books of the Berlin theologian Starck, who had written about the origin and history of the superstition. I told Mr. Munz my opinion on the matter, and he announced it to the public in the 'Neue Freie Presse.' That is how I got into the skirmish."

At the turn of the fifteenth and sixteenth centuries, many towns sought to expel the Jews, which was achieved, for example, in Karlovy Vary, Cheb, Pilsen, Ceske Budejovice, and Louny. Jews did not return until the second half of the nineteenth century. In any case, the Jewish settlement shifted significantly from large towns to smaller ones, sometimes even to the countryside. On the other hand, during the reigns of Maximilian II or Rudolf II, the Jewish communities did not have to fear attacks from the rulers, quite the contrary. It had its pragmatic roots: the Renaissance rulers needed the goods and money of Jewish merchants and bankers for their costly court, for the wars with the Turks, and eventually for the battles with the Bohemian Estates.

In the first half of the eighteenth century, government decrees reintroduced the obligation to live in ghettos. Maria Theresa, the only female ruler of the Hapsburg Empire, even tried to expel the Jewish population from the Bohemian lands. Only the reforms of her son Joseph II brought about a relaxation in policy. In 1781, the obligation for Jews to wear a special label was abolished, and they were allowed to attend all types of domestic higher education, including universities, except for theological universities.

Jews did not gain full equality until 1867 with the promulgation of the so-called December Constitution. Only a few years later, however, new anti-Semitic movements and parties began to emerge in Central Europe that fundamentally questioned the possibility of integrating Jews into mainstream society. According to Holocaust.cz, "What at first seemed like an absurd, medieval, inappropriate and ephemeral phenomenon soon became a firm part of European politics and world and social views." Germany, and Berlin

in particular, became an important center of anti-Semitic opinion in the late 1870s and early 1880s. A few decades later, in 1925 and 1926, Adolf Hitler published Mein Kampf, *a book dominated by fanatical anti-Semitism, which became the unadulterated bible of Nazism. In January 1933, the same Hitler became Chancellor of Germany.*

My mother's family was fortunate to live in Prague. During the Kristallnacht (known as the Night of Broken Glass) of November 9-10, 1938, in Nazi Germany and the annexed Austria, the Nazis unleashed another wave of violence against the Jewish population: synagogues were burned, and shops were destroyed in the Sudeten regions of Czechoslovakia: Karlovy Vary, Sokolov, Liberec, Opava, and other places. Many Jewish families fled further inland, to the territory of the encircled Czechoslovakia. Some 17,000 Jews fled their homes, but many were later arrested by the Nazis and sent to concentration camps.

The motto of the Second Czechoslovakian Republic was "Small but Ours." But it was no longer the democratic country that could set an example for neighboring countries. Society was becoming more radicalized, more nationalistic. And the culprit for the demise of the First Republic was being sought. For the far right, it was the Jews. In some radical newspapers, for example, there were articles about Jews being the most sophisticated pickpockets, pimps, or pornography dealers. It was also a popular theme that Jews abhorred honest physical labor. There were general debates about how to solve the "Jewish Question" (What do we do with the Jews?), how to strictly separate Czechs from Jews, and how to set up Jewish schools in the ghettos. Some of the businessmen rejoiced that the Germans were taking over Jewish-owned businesses and putting them in Czech hands. Indeed, the Second Republic government also promised a quick solution to the Jewish Question and began to lay off state employees of Jewish origin. (Jews were also losing their jobs in other fields.)

What must my grandfather and grandmother have thought about this? How concerned were they about what would follow? Did they worry about how to protect their property?

It didn't take long for the Jewish Question to be taken up by the occupation administration. In March 1939, the Nazis occupied the rest of the country and declared it the Protectorate of Bohemia and Moravia. The Second Czechoslovakian Republic lasted only 165 days, from September 1938 to March 1939.

For my mother, the worst part of her life began.

Chapter 5

Departure

"Why do we have to move?" asked little Hana, tears streaming down her cheeks. It was the end of April 1940, and my mother was not yet twelve. But the events of recent months had pushed her to grow up prematurely when she did not want to willingly give up her childhood just yet. The environment of relative affluence and carefreeness in which she was raised began to crumble for her. This was especially true after the occupation on March 15, 1939, and the establishment of the Protectorate of Bohemia and Moravia. Life changed quickly.

"We just have to. We have to move," her father replied. He was clearly upset. He didn't know how much he could actually tell his now eleven-year-old daughter, without giving her a hint of how afraid he was of the future. "It's an order, and we just have to obey it," he said in a low voice. "We have to do it in two days," he added. Her father was the most important person in her life during those challenging times; it was him she confided in and from whom she sought support.

The beautiful house in Prague's Smichov district, where my mother spent the unforgettable moments of her childhood, ceased to be her home. The whole family had to leave. They were Jews. The first harassment began in the autumn of 1938, but after the establishment of the Protectorate, events gained momentum. The anti-Jewish laws and regulations that the Nazis had introduced, first in Germany and then in Austria, began to be fully implemented in the newly acquired territory as well. Although the Protectorate government tried to transfer Jewish property into Czech hands, only residuals remained, and the Protectorate underwent severe Germanization.

Additionally, there was harsh anti-Semitism with a strangulation of all rights and freedoms of the Jewish population, which, according to official data from March 1939, numbered more than 118,000. The famous anti-Jewish Nuremberg Laws were first applied in the Protectorate relatively early. In June 1939, the Reich Protector Konstantin von Neurath issued a decree regarding Jewish property.

Jews and Jewish enterprises were forbidden by Neurath's decree to dispose of real estate, real estate rights, economic enterprises and shares therein, securities of all kinds, and to rent land and economic enterprises without the written consent of the Reich Protector. They were ordered to declare agricultural and forest lands, objects made of gold, platinum, silver, precious stones, pearls, and artistic objects to the German Chief Land Councillors, if the price of individual objects or collections exceeded the amount of 10 thousand crowns. The acquisition of real estate, shares in economic enterprises, securities, and the take-over and re-establishment of economic establishments was prohibited. The Reich Protector appointed Aryan administrators in Jewish enterprises who were subject to his supervision and order. (Karny, *The Final Solution*)

For Hana and all her immediate family and relatives, the new Protectorate-established conditions meant a shocking life change. Their daily routine had taken a completely different turn. She knew, of course, that she and other children in her family were Jews, but it was never an obstacle. Not even at school. Actually, no one had addressed it. Jew or non-Jew, no one cared. Children dealt with friendship according to other criteria. I know from the stories of our relatives that my mother had many friends in her youth. But that also changed during the occupation. The life she had once known was a hard contrast with the reality of the time. During recess at school, a classmate directly insulted Hana, "You dirty Jew!" It was a shock. Tears welled up in her eyes. She wondered, "Why? Why is she saying that? Why does it bother anyone? What have I done to anybody?" She had no answers; she didn't understand.

Hana also found it difficult to come to terms with the beginning of the 1940 school year when she was no longer allowed to attend school because she was a Jew. "Verboten! [Forbidden!]" Hana thus lost her friends, a part of her childhood, and important experiences that significantly mold a person's character and personality. Fortunately, her father had some connections and at least managed to arrange secret lessons for small groups of Jewish pupils in the parents' flats. The parents hired Jewish teachers who were out of work, and the flats were frequently rotated to avoid discovery by the Nazi authorities. If they were found out, all involved would be immediately deported to a concentration camp.

Acquaintances also helped Hana's father to take care of him and his family. He was far from the only Jewish citizen to lose his job. Doctors, lawyers, and other professions were suddenly out of work. But the family stuck together and supported each other, all the more so in these evil times. Bad news came from all sides. And it wasn't just the Nazis who intensified anti-Semitic policy. The Czech fascists were also very active, especially at the beginning of the Protectorate. For example, in August 1939, strong anti-Jewish riots were reported in Brno, where many Jews were brutally attacked and beaten. The fascists burned the synagogue in Jihlava, damaged the synagogue in Dobris, and attacked the Jewish inhabitants in Pribram. Fortunately, there was no widespread support for this antagonistic behavior. Czech gendarmes (police) intervened against such anti-Semitic rioters, and the general public did not approve of them.

However, the system of discriminatory measures was constantly expanding and strengthening. Beginning in February 1940, people of Jewish origin were required to have a large red "J" on their identity card, i.e., the initial letter of the German Jude—Jew. Later, in the autumn of 1941, the wearing of the yellow Star of David on clothing was compulsory.

> The yellow star on his breast was the mark of Cain. People have turned away from us quite often. Our old friends suddenly didn't want to know us. Parents forbade their children to associate with me. Today I think that it was probably not due to their anti-Semitism, but rather to their fear of being labeled as friends of the Jews. On the other hand, however, there were people who, on the contrary, helped us. The neighbors from the house where we lived invited me to lunch every day. ("Memoirs of Jan Spira" *Memory of Nations* website)

The public space for Jewish inhabitants throughout the Protectorate was shrinking, which Hana felt firsthand. For example, she could no longer just go play in any park as she did before the occupation. According to Nazi regulations, Jews in Prague were initially not allowed to enter Stromovka (Prague's central park), then this ban was extended to all public orchards, gardens, forests, to the Vltava embankment between the Hlavkuv and Railway Bridges, and to an increasing number of streets, especially in the city center. Jews were not allowed to visit theaters, cinemas, libraries, sports venues, swimming pools, public baths, or entertainment centers. If they traveled by tram, a space was reserved for them on one platform of the last car. It was the same on the railways, where Jews were allowed to ride only in the last carriage, and then later restricted to the last compartment of the last carriage. Jews were forbidden to enter waiting rooms or station restaurants. They were allowed to use the post office only between one and three in the afternoon, and only at one location on Ostrovni Street in the center of Prague.

Further restrictions were enforced. Jews also had a strictly defined time for shopping; originally it was two periods of two hours, but later reduced to only between three and five in the afternoon. Jews had reduced food rations, the aforementioned Jan Spira recalled that he and his Jewish father had food coupons only for bread and potatoes. However, his mother was not Jewish, which afforded them some opportunities. "We got meat and fat from my mother's food stamps. But that wasn't enough, so my mother had to do what wasn't allowed. She profiteered. She traded jewelry for food. Everything of value in the war she exchanged for food. What really saved me was that I used to go to my neighbors' house for lunch for a long time," Spira said after the war.

Hagibor was a gathering space that, under normal circumstances, afforded citizens a variety of outdoor activities. For Jewish children in Prague, Hagibor became their last sanctuary and place of refuge. They could meet and play, often coming here from remote parts of the capital and often on foot. Whether my mother also went there, I could not determine, but it's possible. Entertainment for children was organized by the legendary Jewish teacher and athlete Fredy

Hirsch, who emigrated from Nazi Germany to Czechoslovakia in 1935. Hagibor provided a sense of normalcy for children, even if just for a moment. For children, Fredy Hirsch became a symbol of hope, at least for a while, he managed to create a climate like in the normal world. Whether it was in Hagibor, Theresienstadt (Terezin), or Auschwitz, Hirsch instilled a sense of pride in people.

> He himself was a very proud person who never submitted to the Germans, who talked to them in an incredible way, almost arrogantly. I witnessed this myself. Sometimes I was amazed that the SS, even though they reached for their guns, never used them against Fredy, at most, they beat him. Perhaps it was because Fredy had something of a tamer— he looked the SS in the eyes and maybe influenced them. (Ruzickova, *Sto Zazraku*)

Hagibor operated for children until 1943. Later, a labor camp for mica processing was established there. Several thousand people passed through it, and, from what I have read, among them were the famous Czech actor Oldrich Novy and the lesser-known writer Ondrej Sekora, whose wives were Jewish.

By that time, however, Hirsch was dead. In December 1941, he was among the first to be deported to the emerging ghetto in Terezin. Even there, he tried to help young prisoners. In September 1943, he was transported to Auschwitz, where he managed to establish a children's block for about 500 children in the part called the Terezin family camp. Even within Auschwitz, Terezin arrivals were separated from everyone else and, in essence, had their own camp-within-a-camp. In March 1944, the resistance movement in the extermination camp tried to persuade him to become the leader of the uprising, because most of the prisoners from the family camp were to end up in the gas chambers. But Hirsch probably committed suicide, likely poisoning himself.

At the beginning of 1940, Hana and her family were still living in their villa in Smichov. It was at the height of Jewish emigration. At that time, it was still possible to leave the Protectorate, even if it meant giving up one's property. The occupation authorities even set up a special emigration office. More than 25,000 Jewish residents took advantage of this, heading to Palestine, the United States, South America, and China.

Most Jews were able to emigrate until June of 1940. After that date, the numbers dramatically decreased. While 19,016 Jews legally emigrated from the Protectorate in 1939 and another 6,176 in 1940, emigrant numbers dropped to 535 in 1941, 273 in 1942, and only 93 in 1943. Thus, a total of 26,093 Jews legally emigrated from the Protectorate. This total does not include those who left illegally, above all to Poland, and, after its occupation, to the territory of the Slovak state. All considered, it is estimated that about 30,000 Jews escaped from the Protectorate.

Hana's father was likely considering emigration, even though it was probably too late. I discovered a contemporary police report from March 21, 1942, which indicated he was arrested by gendarmes at Prague's Main Railway Station. "Rudolf Klein was brought in because he was unreasonably lingering at the Main Station near the arrival of trains, which is forbidden to Jews," the protocol read. I am convinced, knowing the risk of being arrested and punished, that he went to the station to find out if there was a departing train for the whole family to take. Where it was headed, I'll probably never know. At least some members of our family, two of my grandfather's brothers, managed to escape before 1939.

But let's go back two more years. In the spring of 1940, Hana's father came to the family villa with the announcement that the authorities had ordered them to move out. He had been expecting something like this and had been preparing for it, as I later learned from relatives and acquaintances who survived the Holocaust. Although he had to relinquish many valuable items due to racial laws, he still managed to take away a considerable number of items in the evenings with the help of Aunt Anna and Uncle William: paintings, books, carpets, and porcelain. Where the possessions eventually ended up, even the surviving relatives did not know. Hana was made ready for the move quite quickly. Her priority was not to forget her favorite doll. It was one remaining connection to her fleeting childhood.

On April 26, 1940, the Kleins sadly left the home that had been their family domain for seven years. Their new home was a two-room apartment in what was then Durdikova Street (today known as Rosickych Street). When they arrived, two unknown families were already staying there. Hana sat down on the floor in the corner of the kitchen and couldn't believe that they were now living with strangers. But there was nothing to be done. Her father collaborated with other adults on the arrangement of the household and the best possible division of living space. In the end, they solved it by having Hana and her older brother Petr stay in the kitchen with another son of one of the families, and the parents divided the two remaining rooms. The living arrangements were not unlike those cramped quarters described by Anne Frank in her diary recounting her family's experiences with the van Pels family when they went into hiding from the Nazis in Amsterdam during WWII.

At that time, Hana's father got a job managing the sewers, and in the winter, he was clearing snow. He left the apartment very early every morning, returning in the evening very tired. Still, he found enough strength in himself to have fun with both children. For Hana, it was always the best part of the day. She loved her father very much. Hana's mother had never cooked in the family villa before, but now she had to learn quickly. And above all, she had to cook with what little the family got on food stamps or from elsewhere. In the kitchen, she took turns with the other women. Sometime after the move, Hana's father arranged for her to learn secretly again in small children's clubs at someone's apartment. It wasn't every day, but when it was possible, Hana was glad. It was a welcome distraction from their distressing situation.

The Kleins seemed to be getting used to a spartan life when the next order to move came. And again, they were given only two days to prepare. Fortunately, there was almost nothing to pack this time; they were ready quickly. Hana gripped her doll tightly again and was ready. It was the end of 1940. The holidays were approaching, a festive time, but there was not much mood for any celebration.

The Klein family set off for a new address, this time to a several-story, tall, corner house on Dlouha Street. They walked. Hana knew the street. Her father had once showed her the Aschermann Café here, where he sometimes met with his business partners or friends before the war. This time, however, no one thought of visiting the café. Rather, they had thoughts of what awaited them in their new location, and they wondered who would live there with them this time. When the front door slammed shut behind them, the first impression was quite attractive. The beautiful mosaic on the entrance hall floor and the ornate railing above the staircase was impressive. But what would come next? They were supposed to report to the apartment of the Tuma family, who welcomed them warmly—accommodation for the Kleins in one of the three rooms was already prepared. The daily routine was organized similarly to the previous housing. Coincidentally, Hana's Uncle Karel, his wife, and son, Ruda, also lived with a family on Dlouha Street. Karel's son was seven years older than Hana.

It was natural to have questions. Hana immediately wondered how long they would remain there before they had to move again or if her father could secure another teaching group. But all these thoughts were overwhelmed by harsh reality. At the beginning of 1941 came a very hard winter; the temperature dropped well below freezing, and there was much snow in the streets of Prague. Hana's father had work clearing the snow which was hard manual labor that he wasn't used to. It overwhelmed him, even though he never complained about it at home. Hana couldn't help but notice how tired he was in the evenings. Moreover, there was little food and a shortage of coal and other fuel for heating. The apartment was cold. Everyone was hungry. Hana couldn't have known it, but she was actually being trained for her life in the Terezin Ghetto.

The Third Historical Stop

The Center of Jewish Prague

Even before the occupation, many Jewish families lived on Dlouha Street, where there were also the headquarters of various Jewish institutions. For example, house No. 33 housed the Transporthilfe or Hilfsdienst, i.e., the auxiliary transport service. Its volunteers, from the ranks of Jewish youth, helped the citizens who were included in the transports with packing their luggage and accompanied them to the assembly point.

Dlouha Street was also the seat of the Jewish Labor Center, which helped Jewish men who were not allowed to practice their profession due to anti-Jewish regulations. They were assigned to various auxiliary jobs, such as snow removal, or they worked as unskilled workers on construction sites. Dlouha Street also housed the editorial office of the weekly Jewish Letters (Judisches Nachrichtenblatt), published by the Prague Jewish Religious Community, and the Zionist Maccabi Centre.

There was a warehouse, the so-called Treuhandstelle, a special department of the Prague Jewish Religious Community, whose task was to take care of the furnishings of Prague apartments left by deported inhabitants. The agenda was overseen by the Central Office for Jewish Emigration, later renamed the Central Office for the Settlement of Jewish Questions. In this warehouse antiques, refrigerators, suitcases, but also books or sheet music were stored. Other warehouses were, for example, on Maiselova, Siroky, Hastalska, Dusni, or Jerusalem Streets—often in closed synagogues.

Until its dissolution in 1941, No. 41 housed the Central Zionist Union—Palestinian Authority, which brought together Zionist organizations and prepared those interested in emigrating to Palestine. Until 1943, the Aschermann Café operated on the ground floor of the building, probably the last Prague café accessible to Jewish citizens during the occupation.

Not far from Dlouha Street is Prague's Jewish Town or Josefov, which was once the largest Jewish settlement in Europe. Since the tenth century, Jewish merchants first settled closer to Prague Castle, on the site of today's Lesser Town, but in the twelfth century, the Jewish population began to move to the other bank of the Vltava. The original settlement gradually grew into the Jewish Town—with its own council, judiciary, education, extensive self-government, and, of course, synagogues. It was separated from the rest of the city by a wall.

At the time of the greatest boom, 1.9 thousand people lived on an area of 305 thousand square feet.

At the end of the 1880s, the quarter was sanitized, and several hundred medieval houses and two dozen streets were demolished. Only a few buildings from the ghetto have been preserved, but Josefov is still an important European monument. For example, the Old-New Synagogue from the last quarter of the thirteenth century, which was the main synagogue of the Prague Jewish Community, is the oldest synagogue on the Old Continent. The Old Jewish Cemetery is also a monument of world importance. The exact date of its foundation is unknown, but the oldest known tombstone dates from April 25, 1439, and it belongs to the famous scholar and poet Rabbi Avigdor Kara. People were buried in the cemetery until 1787. At present, there are 12,000 tombstones.

During the Nazi occupation, Jews were deported to concentration camps. Before the start of the transports in the autumn of 1941, almost 40,000 Jewish inhabitants lived in Prague, but only 7,540 survived.

One evening Hana overheard her mother and father talking quietly. They looked worried, even turning their backs on the children so they wouldn't be heard, but even so, Hana heard the word *transport*. In the months that followed, she heard it more and more often. But she did not realize how it might affect them. Neither her father nor her mother wanted to talk about it, but she learned from her roommates in the apartment on Dlouha Street that there was a plan to transport Jews to the east, to Poland.

Indeed, in the autumn of 1941, the first transport left the Protectorate for the Lodz Ghetto in Poland. Of the 5,000 people who arrived there, only 277 survived to see the end of the war. Of course, Hana didn't know that. But she was increasingly gripped by a fear of the unknown. Now it was no longer a worry about what other residence they would move into, but whether they would end up somewhere else much farther away.

"Papa, what's going to happen to us?" asked the now thirteen-year-old girl. Of course, her father constantly comforted her and assured her that everything would be fine; she need not worry about anything, and that she would definitely return to her house in Smichov eventually. But he had to realize at this point it was likely that his daughter did not believe him much anymore.

At the beginning of November 1941, a ghetto was established in Terezin. The ghettos were designated areas of towns and cities run by German occupiers but often self-governed by Jews. Those Jews who served in this supervisory capacity were still prisoners and still under the authority of the Nazis. Ghettos were enclosed by walls or barriers, and Jews and others were forced to live in often over-crowded and very unsanitary conditions. They were a "holding place" before people were deported to the killing camps (such as Auschwitz) where exterminations took place.

Even Hana's father knew that going to Terezin meant life would be worse rather than better. The number of transports increased at a rapid pace. The Kleins learned from their friends that Aunt Anna, with her husband and son, had already left for Terezin. The question was no longer whether they would be transported, but when. In the spring of 1942, the Kleins received a notification that they were being included in a transport to Terezin Ghetto at the beginning of May.

The horror was becoming all too real.

Chapter 6

Assembly at Radio Trade Fair

ow was that final night "at home"? Hardly anyone slept properly. Gloomy thoughts ran through everyone's mind and kept them all awake. Hana was lying on her side, her doll pressed to her face, and she whispered, "You have to be strong. Don't worry, we'll all stick together, just like my Daddy said." Eventually, she finally managed to fall asleep . . . but not for long. Her parents were already dressed to leave when they went to wake Hana and her brother Petr the next morning. The sun was shining, and something small to eat was already prepared and placed on the table. But the children didn't feel like eating. In recent days, Marta Klein had been gathering general food supplies and small baked loaves of bread so that no one would be hungry on the way. She wasn't sure if there would be some food at their unknown next destination.

Hana sat on the edge of the bed with her backpack strapped on her shoulders and a small suitcase at her feet. There were still the last few moments left here together. Then her father smiled slightly to project some air of pleasantness to the situation. "Let's go," he said softly. They walked out into the hallway, and Mr. Klein locked the apartment that had been home for the family for over a year.

It was May 8, 1942. They descended a staircase adorned by an ornate banister that Hana had always admired. The whole house was still asleep, with only the sound of their boots reverberating on the steps. They were already in front of the house at No. 9 Dlouha Street, but Hana did not look back. What might she have been thinking at that moment? On the street, they were meeting numerous families who were heading to the same place as the Klein family: the Radio Trade Fair Assembly Center near the Holesovice Trade Fair Palace.

People all greeted each other quietly. But the men couldn't even remove their hats, as was customary, because they were carrying suitcases or holding children. Among the crowds of people with the yellow star on their coats, non-Jewish residents of Prague rushed to work. Some of those on the sidewalks only glanced briefly at the travelers with their luggage, wishing they were gone, but others at least slowed down and raised their hands in greeting and respectful acknowledgement. The Kleins were approaching the Aschermann Café when they saw Uncle Karel's family. They had received a summons to the assembly point for today as well. The Aschermann Café was an important meeting place for Prague Jews in the 1930s, especially during the Nazi occupation. Until 1942 it was the only place in Prague where Jews could meet. It was located in Prague 1, the Old Town (today's No. 33 Dlouha Street/Long Street). It also shared spaces with Prague's Jewish Cultural Community, including the Labor Office, the Palestine Office, and some others. The café doesn't exist anymore.

Hana's father talked to Karel for a moment, and then he informed the rest of the family that they were all going to Terezin. Hopefully it wouldn't be as bad there as in Poland, he thought to himself. Slowly, the family approached the tram stop at Dlouha Street. The tram arrived half empty, but soon it filled up with Jewish families, heading toward the Radio Trade Fair Palace. Next to it, several years before the war, exhibition pavilions were built for trade shows showcasing mostly radios. After many years of neglect, the Nazis transformed the dilapidated buildings into the largest deportation center, not only in Prague, but in the entire Protectorate.

At each stop, more Jewish families boarded. Mr. Klein checked his watch periodically to make sure they would arrive at the appointed hour. At the Radio Trade Fair's tram stop, most people exited the trolley cars. People with suitcases, backpacks, and other belongings headed for the entrance to the buildings, separated from the surrounding area by a wooden fence reinforced with barbed wire. Everywhere there were gendarmes and SS men (elite political soldiers of the Nazi party) yelling at the arriving masses of now prisoners. For Hana and the others, it was the beginning of what was to become everyday life under constant orders and prohibitions.

People crowded in front of the main entrances to the fairgrounds, and nervousness grew. Some children, but also women, cried, and strict Nazi orders were heard. The assembly area in the complex of the former Radio Trade Fair was established not long after Reinhard Heydrich took office as acting Reich Protector of Bohemia and Moravia. It is a place with a turbulent history. During the Nazi occupation it served as a collection camp for the Jewish inhabitants of Prague who were called up for transport to Lodz (Poland) and

Terezin. For many Jewish families, a stay in these premises represented the last moments they could spend together. For the efficient
organization and secrecy of the entire trial, the Nazis chose the run-
down cottages of this complex, which until then had been used by
the Gestapo. The decisive factor was certainly the proximity of the
Prague-Bubny railway station. It was in operation from October 1941
until July 1943.

Nobody knew what awaited them behind the gate. Hana gripped
her father's hand increasingly tighter, clutching her doll in her other
hand.

"Why are you taking the doll with you?" her brother Petr asked
her several times in the authoritative and condescending tone that
older siblings sometimes use with their younger sisters or brothers.
"You're almost fourteen, girls don't play with dolls anymore," he
laughed at her.

Hana gave him a sad look and made it clear that she wasn't going
to give up her doll. It was as if she were holding her childhood in her
arms, which was about to unknowingly slip from her. They moved
slowly in a long line toward the main gate. Hana watched the children who, like her, did not move from their parents, clinging to
them like ticks, while some mothers embraced their smaller children
and infants in their arms. Many were getting overheated because
they were wearing several layers of clothes, which saved them from
the limitations on the weight of their personal luggage, which was
not allowed to exceed a total of fifty kilograms (about 110 pounds).
Finally, the entire Klein family reached the main gate and entered.

Here, the SS were already in charge. The Kleins entered one of
the houses, and Rudolf had to first report, in German, the transport
numbers of all the family members to one of them. Each transport
to Terezin was assigned a letter code. The preparation and execu-
tion of the transports were largely the task of the Prague Jewish
Administration and its "Transport Department." Those who were
selected for a transport were notified by messenger and received an
identification number. In the case of my family, I discovered their
transport number (letter code) to Terezin was Au, and their personal
numbers were 755, 756, 757, and 758. For the duration of their stay

in Terezin Ghetto, these codes became part of their name and had to be included in all official communications.

Many people gathered in the barrack: young and old, some on crutches, babies, but also children of Hana's age. Next, they were in line for the German officer's table. Rudolf Klein answered questions, and then he still had to hand over some personal belongings, including the keys to his last apartment. His daughter noticed the SS man leading them to where the family must proceed. She turned her head in that direction, but she couldn't imagine having to proceed through the wall of human bodies. Nevertheless, they pushed their way through the crowd of people and among all kinds of luggage; her father was looking for the rectangular shapes with numbers painted on the ground. That's how they got to their new "home": four rectangles, measuring three by six feet. On the ground, a torn and smelly straw mattress was prepared for everyone.

They sat down on it, needing to recover and digest the previous events, and at which point, Hana burst into tears. Petr was also struggling with his emotional distress, holding his head in his hands. "We'll get through this, we'll get through this," their parents comforted them. But it didn't help much. They were desperate themselves trying to control their feelings. All that was left of a decent, well-to-do family were just four figures sitting on dirty straw. They felt they were losing their dignity. They felt like animals.

After the family was able to compose themselves, Hana's mother, Marta, took food out of her backpack. The butter on the bread may have melted, but the jam lasted and came in handy for the children. It tasted like the best meal ever. Hana held back her tears and tried to encourage herself. "If someone is hungry and wants to eat, the place where we eat it doesn't matter," she told herself.

Rudolf Klein went to another Nazi official at the other end of the barrack. Once again, he had to make his way among the throng of frightened people. He had to fill out more forms, pick up his food stamps, and the SS officer again ordered him to hand over whatever valuables he still had on him. His watch had to go. The officer threatened Klein with severe punishment if additional valuables were found on him. There was nothing of monetary value left from among their belongings. Nothing at all.

Hana sat down, leaned against the wall, and opened her book. But she couldn't really focus on reading, her mind jumbled with thoughts of what might happen next? Do Mommy and Daddy know? But they do not want to tell us because they don't want to scare me and Petr? She closed her eyes and remembered Daddy, how elegant he had been before the occupation, perfectly dressed, well-liked, and respected. He had many friends, and when the whole family didn't go away for the weekend, he used to go to the Aschermann Café in Dlouha Street, or the Louvre Café on Narodni trida (National Boulevard).

Rudolf Klein was strict with his children, but not as much as his wife, Marta. All he had to do was look at his children, and they knew what they should or shouldn't do. He didn't like tardiness; they always had to be everywhere on time. He instructed them how to be polite and respect other people, that they shouldn't lie but should tell the truth.

Hana's thoughts turned to her mother. Marta was a lady who didn't have an expansive wardrobe but still dressed very modern, and she dressed her children the same way. She was a stickler for order. As a little girl, Hana always had to put her toys away before proceeding to something else. Sometimes her mother grew frustrated with her, but they resolved any issues between them without intervention and with Marta kindly explaining to her daughter the cause of her disappointment. Mrs. Klein usually avoided telling her husband about any disagreements or tension; instead, she bestowed a great deal of praise on Petr and Hana in front of Rudolf. Before the war, when her children went shopping with her, they often stopped at her favorite confectionery, U Mysaka, near Wenceslas Square. There were goodies in the form of many different pastries. Marta usually had one piece with her black coffee! At home, she pushed her children to study often; she saw knowledge as the basis of good character and personal development. There was always the expectation that her children had to finish all of their homework and other school duties before they were allowed to go out to see their friends.

Hana sat on the straw mattress and tried to understand what her parents could have done to the Germans to deserve such treatment. She put the book down without reading a single page. Her father appeared, and with him came Uncle Karel and cousin Rudolf, whom everyone called Ruda. They met at the clerk's desk, dealing with formalities that seemed to have no end. They would continue again the next day. The same forms had to be filled out once again. Same procedures, same questions. Up to a thousand people were crammed into several barracks, and when all the official duties were done, they would continue. The word was out that it might take several days. Hana leaned over to her mother and whispered that she had to go to the bathroom. Together with Petr and Ruda, they went to find a place to relieve themselves. They discovered this place after a long time, and there was a terrible smell in the air. Hana pinched her nose and went inside. She immediately ran out again. Not there! No toilets, just buckets lined up against one wall. Eventually, Hana returned because she had no choice.

Night was approaching. Everyone was tired, but neither Hana nor the other family members wanted to sleep yet. The neighbors were talking; several small children were crying; there was even laughter from somewhere. Finally, the tiredness overcame them. There was no evening hygiene; they just took off their shoes and went to bed. Sleep did not last long. "Achtung, Achtung! [Attention!]" rang through the barracks, followed by some German announcement that Hana did not understand and did not care to hear. She wanted to sleep. But the "Achtung" announcement was repeated several more times during the night.

And then it was morning, and some of them hadn't slept much. The SS men were walking among the people lying on the ground, ordering them to address more official business. There was the reiteration that they had to give up all money or jewelry. This had been demanded countless times before. Breakfast followed, which consisted of watery coffee and a piece of stale, rotten, and moldy bread. Then it was off to the washroom, where, to everyone's delight, real lukewarm water was running. The day passed slowly again. It was a very boring time for the children, and some of them went to the yard where they tried to entertain themselves. Hana looked around to see if she could recognize any friends, but she didn't know anyone there.

Time for lunch. The food was given out in one of the barracks, where there was a long line. One of the guards took the meal tickets and checked the numbers so that no one would go twice and handed each person a bowl. Once each person reached the window of the barrack, the cook threw in one old potato and covered it with some brown stuff that couldn't even be called gravy.

The afternoon followed the same pattern and tone as the morning. Mr. Klein was taking care of some official business again. But he never complained about it. He had been gone for a long time, so his children went looking for him, even though their mother tried to persuade them not to. They came across several groups of elderly people who were in ill health, being looked after by a few volunteers. They were lying in an adjacent barrack, where the heat was unbearable, and the air was encumbered by a stench. The children failed to find their father, so they returned "home." Their father was already there. In the evening, the SS men came again, walking among the straw mattresses, shouting at some people, even beating them. Hana was fearful and hid behind her father.

The next day, more of the same. Time dragged incredibly slowly. It was very hot and pungent in the barracks. Klein was running errands again. Marta added half a slice of bread from the dwindling supplies to the insufficient lunch. Cousin Ruda arrived in the afternoon, and Hana and Petr went out to the yard with him. Here, it was not as hot, which suited most of them. Some of the boys played soccer. They didn't have an actual ball, so they took a large can wrapped in a cloth and kicked it around.

"How much longer are we going to be here?" Hana asked her father before going to bed. He couldn't honestly answer her.

"They didn't tell us that at the tables, but I don't think it will be much longer," he told her.

The next morning, they were startled by the screams of the SS men. "Aufstehen! [Get up!]" Suddenly, there was no time for anything. Breakfast was halted abruptly, and hundreds of people had to gather in the courtyard. Hana looked around. What would happen next? The SS men with rifles in their hands lined them up in rows according to their numbers, which each person had to wear around their neck. People held their luggage or put it on the ground. Long minutes passed, and nothing happened. Then one of the SS men stepped up onto a makeshift platform and began to speak to the hundreds of assembled and confused people in a loud, hoarse voice. Hana stood quite close to the soldier. She was struck by his black, polished boots. At this time, she was oblivious to the idea that soon this would be the daily routine for her and most of those around her. Silence reigned.

"Today, a new chapter of your life begins," the SS man spoke in German. "You are going to Theresienstadt, where everything has been prepared for you, and where you will share your life in peace and comfort with the members of your race."

When Hana asked her father what the SS man had said, he replied, "We are going to Terezin. Everything will be alright, don't worry." He squeezed her hand tighter.

It was Tuesday, May 12, 1942. The Klein family, in a crowd with other Jewish residents, once again passed through the gate through which they had entered three days before. It was still early in the morning, and the streets were nearly empty.

The new chapter ahead seemed ominous.

Chapter 7

On Transport

The long human serpent set off on its march toward Bubny Train Station. The journey was about 3,000 feet long. For most of the 1,000 prisoners (of which only 62 survived), it was the last time they walked along the streets of Prague. People were no longer referred to by their names; their identities were now reduced to numbers. Hana couldn't help but notice how some of the older people had to be physically supported by their closest friends or acquaintances during the march. The pace was faltering, and the Nazi guards tried to force those who were lagging behind to move more quickly by shouting sharply. The people were frightened and horrified, with their heads down, but they just couldn't go any faster. Some of them already looked very shabby; they were thin, and their clothes were dirty. But some still walked with their heads up proudly, not wanting to show their humiliation or their fear of things to come. The march was supervised by Czech gendarmes alongside the SS.

The front of the procession soon reached the grounds of the Bubny Train Station in Holesovice, with its distinctive gray station building. The area in front of the building was quickly filled with arriving people. Several cars were already lined up on the tracks; dark smoke was rising from the locomotive's smokestack, and the train was ready with its doors open for the prisoners to enter. For most of them, the destination was still unknown. There was no time to look around. The SS men shouted instructions into the crowd, poked the arrivals with their rifles and directed them by their assigned numbers to the appropriately marked train cars. There was a tense feeling of organized chaos. Children were crying once again, holding tightly to their parents. Many older people were not able to climb into the wagon without assistance because the first step was too high from the ground. This obstacle caused an overwhelming backup while many people were pushing from behind. The SS men were striking the prisoners even more severely at this point, which did not remedy the situation. The older and physically handicapped prisoners had an especially difficult time moving without the support of others.

All the way to the station, no one spoke. Hana whispered something in her brother's ear and pointed to a carriage, indicating their numbers. Hana and Petr got on first; their parents handed the luggage up to them and then followed. Once inside the train cars, the calculation of the planning was evident: the seats were numbered with the prisoners' transport numbers. Everything was seemingly well-organized. The passengers put their backpacks on the overhead top shelves and slid their suitcases under the seats. They took off their coats, but they had to keep the tags with their personal transport numbers 755, 756, 757, and 758 hanging around their necks. Cooler air came in through the open windows. Rudolf and Marta sat down with their children sandwiched between them. At that moment, they had no idea that they would never return to Prague nor would they even live to see the liberation. They tried to calm down so that their children would be calmer too, but their hearts were pounding. More people were getting into the carriage, but Hana didn't notice much. She leaned her head on her father's shoulder and fell asleep. The noise of people boarding slowly died down. A few more German commands came from outside, and the doors banged shut. It had taken about an hour for hundreds of people to board and get organized. The SS men were anxious and irritated. Finally, the transport was ready to leave for Terezin.

The Fourth Historical Stop

The Train Station for the Departure from Normal Life

Construction of the train station, on the site of the former village of Bubny, was initiated in 1866, and it began operating two years later, at the end of April 1868. However, the current appearance of the station dates from 1868. Originally the station was called Bubny, but it has had its current name of Prague-Bubny since 1941. It was in this year that transports to the ghettos in Lodz and Terezin began to leave from this station. Most of the tens of thousands of people who boarded the transports never returned. Eva Erbenova was lucky. Very lucky. She headed from Prague-Bubny Station to Terezin when she was eleven. She ended up in the Auschwitz extermination camp, but at the end of the war she managed to escape the death march. After the liberation, she moved to Israel and returned to the infamous train station in 2017 to commemorate the transports.

> People from normal life were leaving here—doctors, lawyers, professors who were very well dressed and didn't know they were going to their deaths. My dad was an optimist. He said that Hitler, the maniac, the madman, couldn't last for too long. They took everything from us? Then we'll go back, work and build a new life. We left as people with dignity, well dressed, very civil, on an ordinary passenger train. You really didn't think you were going to your death. (Escape Story by Eva Erbenova)

Since 2015, a monumental object by an academic sculptor, Ales Vesely, commemorates the transports of Jewish residents from the Bubny Train Station, entitled The Gate of No Return. (Fifty thousand Jewish people from the Protectorate were deported from this train station.) The sculpture takes the form of a set of 65 feet of train tracks raised to the sky. It was unveiled on March 9, 2015, which is also significant. On the night of March 8-9, 1944, 3,792 men, women, and children were gassed in the so-called Terezin family camp in Auschwitz, which was referred to in Birkenau as section BIIb. It was so named because people from the Terezin Ghetto were transported there. At the beginning of March 1944, SS officers told the first large group of prisoners from the family camp that they would be transferred to the Heydebreck forced labor camp. But instead, the trucks headed for the gas chambers. "The prisoners were taken out of the blocks at midnight. The rest of us weren't allowed to move, but we were still paralyzed with terror. In my mother's arms, I finally fell asleep in the morning," Zuzana Ruzickova, who survived the Auschwitz death factory, recalled years later. People who ended up in the gas chambers sang the Czechoslovakian national anthem and Hatikvah, the Jewish anthem, before they died. Since that night in March, the other inhabitants of the Terezin family camp likely would have lived in a state of constant suspicion about what would become of them. Their fears were realized in July 1944, when larger *groups headed to the gas chambers. The fortunate ones were sent to work in other camps. Of the 17,500 prisoners in the family camp, only 1,294 survived.*

More than seventy-five years after that fateful day in May 1942, I, too, walked the entire journey from the Radio Fairgrounds deportation assembly center to the Prague-Bubny Train Station, where my mother and her family went. As I walked in their footsteps, my throat was tight, and I thought about what must have been going through everyone's minds. I walked slowly like the long crowd of people likely did then. At the station, I walked around the building and entered the platform and further on to the tracks, where I believed the train cars were loaded with the prisoners. I narrowed my eyes and pictured the wagons ready to take the Jewish prisoners to Terezin. It was very hard for me to imagine what had occurred here. I "saw" my mother, her brother, and my grandparents.

A moment later, the stationmaster woke me up from my solemn contemplation. He briskly asked me what I was doing there. It was a prohibited area. I explained to him that my mother and her family had left from this point for the Terezin Ghetto in May 1942. I asked him if I could take a small stone from between the tracks, thinking, and perhaps hoping, it was one Hana may have stepped on when she boarded the train. The train conductor's expression softened, and he said that it was quite possible, because the stones between the tracks were probably still from that time. I picked up a dark rock while looking in the direction where the Kleins and so many others had left Prague in May 1942.

There were one thousand other Jews on the train with the Kleins. The transport started to move, then stopped. Nobody knew what was happening at that moment. Those sitting at the windows reported that they saw only SS men. After a few minutes, the train lurched forward, moving again. This time, it didn't stop and picked up speed when Hana woke up. She wondered what it would be like in Terezin.

"Where are we going to sleep tonight?" She turned to both parents. "But we'll still be together, right?" she kept asking. "And will there be school?" She didn't get any answers. Marta took the last of the food supplies out of her backpack and handed them out to her husband and children.

About two hours later, the train stopped. The sign read "Bohusovice nad Ohri," and anxiety over what was next was pervasive.

Chapter 8

Terezin Ghetto

Hana finally fell asleep again on the train ride. But it was not the deep sleep she usually had at home in her comfortable bed. Her mind floated, suspended somewhere between sleep and wakefulness, prodded and poked by feelings of dread. But it was mainly her fear of the unknown that prevented any chance of rest. And when she finally woke up for good, it was due to the assault of sharp screeching brakes. The train was slowly stopping. She peered cautiously out of the window. There was a small station and a sign that read "Bohusovice nad Ohri." The first passengers started to get off the platform. The young helped the weaker ones, and heavy suitcases and other luggage were carefully taken out of the train. The intrusive barking of German commands from men in uniforms was again sounding, "Schnell, schnell! [Quick, quick!]"

The Kleins collected their luggage, rose from their seats, and made their way slowly, in the wake of their fellow passengers, to the exit of the train. It was early afternoon, Saturday, May 12, 1942. The already rather long and dramatic trip loomed large, but it was becoming clear to all that this day of unpleasant and uncertain experiences was far from over. It would forever be etched deep in Hana's memory as the day when the greatest humiliation of her life began, and what would be a personal and tragic turn for her, her brother, her mother, and her father.

The passengers from the train lined up at the station building and once again set off on their march. German commands were still heard all around. Hana turned to glance back and saw that the procession was not holding up very well. The SS clearly did not like this and took more forceful action to achieve faster movement among the prisoners. To the sharp commands they added explosive blows with rifle butts or kicks. Some of the people struggled and could barely stand on their feet, but nobody outwardly seemed to care for them too much. There was little compassion to be found among the marchers for fear of retaliation from the SS.

Hana squeezed her father's hand tighter and quietly asked, "I'm sure we're close, aren't we?" Her father feigned a slight smile, but Hana understood by his expression that even he was unaware of what was in store for them in the next few hours.

It is about a mile and a half from Bohusovice to Terezin. For a healthy person, this is a distance that can be covered in twenty to thirty minutes, however, not for old, sick, and stressed people, who were already half-dead exiting the train cars in Bohusovice that were on the way to the ghetto. The Nazi initially tried to conceal the poorly looking procession of thousands of prisoners from the local civilian population as much as possible. The march on foot to Terezin was just a glimpse of the inhumane treatment inflicted by the Nazis that they attempted to conceal from the world. On many occasions, however, they were not successful. Many contemporary photos survive to reveal several transports of thousands of prisoners marching through the village. As a result, the decision was made to build a new railway track from Bohusovice to Terezin through the Bohusovice gate. Construction began in August 1942, with about 300 prisoners working on it, using 180 tons of iron, 48,000 wooden sleepers, and 5,000 tons of gravel. On the first day of June 1943, the project was completed, and control of the track was handed to the Nazis.

The Klein family still had to walk that distance on the trek to Terezin. It didn't take Hana long to set foot in Terezin Ghetto. She walked along the right side of the column, looking around curiously. As the group was herded past the red brick buildings with their large arched gates opened, Hana perceived what she initially thought was a hallucination likely caused by fatigue. But the sight didn't disappear like a mirage . . . even when she closed and reopened her eyes. She saw death. Dead bodies piled in several layers. A cold shiver ran down her spine. Where on earth are they taking us? It wouldn't be long before the innocent girl would know that death would become a normal part of her life moving forward. She couldn't shake the sight. Piles of corpses. The marchers continued on, but Hana felt disoriented. She could still see death before her eyes. She was only snapped out of her trance by the screams of terror from the people following her. They also saw dead bodies. It was real.

Hana tried to distract herself from what she had just witnessed by desperately scrambling to other thoughts, such as "Where would they sleep tonight?" She was tired, hungry, and thirsty. But the long human serpent continued on its way without any hint of answers to her questions. They walked through cobblestone streets, the tall and lower barracks on either side. The sun was already descending toward the bleak horizon, with the buildings casting long, gruesome shadows, adding to the overall unfathomable atmosphere.

The Fifth Historical Stop

Terezin Ghetto

Terezin Ghetto became an important part of the Nazi Final Solution to the Jewish Question that culminated with six million people killed on the European continent. It was neither a "ghetto" as such nor strictly a concentration camp. Terezin served as a "settlement," a collection camp, transit camp, and a concentration camp, and thus had recognizable features of both ghettos and concentration camps. From here, the Jewish prisoners were eventually transported to extermination camps in the East, such as Auschwitz, Treblinka, Maly Trostinec, Majdanek, and Chelmo. At the same time, it was a place where large groups of Jews of retirement age were sent from various European countries—Terezin was also a so-called old-age ghetto. And it also fulfilled a decimation function—tens of thousands of men, women, and children died there. Terezin was founded in 1780 by the Habsburg Emperor Joseph II in the Elbe basin at the confluence of the Elbe and Ohre rivers as a garrison/fortress town for 5,600 soldiers, named in honor of his mother, Maria Theresa. It is located only about thirty miles from Prague. The ghetto existed for three and a half years, between November 24, 1941 and May 9, 1945. It mainly served four purposes for the Nazis:

1. *It served as a transit camp for Czech Jews whom the Germans were continuously deporting to killing centers and forced-labor camps in the East.*

2. *It served as an incarceration center for certain categories of German, Austrian, Czech, Danish, Slovakian, Hungarian, and Dutch Jews, based on their age, disability, past military service, or domestic celebrity in the arts and culture.*

3. *It served as a holding pen for Jews in the above-mentioned groups. It was expected that poor conditions would hasten the death of the prisoners (35,409 were murdered there), until the Nazis could deport the survivors to killing centers in the East (88,129 were deported, most of those to Auschwitz).*

4. *It served an important propaganda function for the Nazi regime. The publicly stated purpose for the deportation of the Jews was their "resettlement to the East" to perform forced labor. Also, it was cynically described as a "spa town" where elderly German Jews could "retire" in safety.*

According to the Nazis, Terezin had many qualities that made it suitable to achieve these purposes: the fortress was cut off from the outside world, and it was built in a strictly symmetrical manner so that it could be easily controlled. There were eleven barracks and other buildings where large numbers of people could be accommodated. A branch of the Prague Gestapo had already been established in the Terezin Small Fortress (about one mile away from Terezin Ghetto) in 1940. If a riot broke out in the ghetto, the SS units from the Small Fortress would quickly be dispatched to intervene. Other SS and Wehrmacht units were in nearby Litomerice, which was across the border from the Protectorate in the Sudeten part of Germany.

The preparations all began on November 24, 1941, when 342 young Jewish men arrived at the Sudeten Barracks in Terezin with the task of preparing the other buildings. Transports began to flow into the ghetto starting November 30, 1941. "By the end of 1942, three-quarters of the entire Jewish population living in the territory of the Protectorate in November 1941 had been 'ghettoized'," wrote Miroslav Karny in his book The Final Solution. *Tens of thousands more arrived from Germany, Austria, the Netherlands, Denmark, Slovakia, and Hungary. The Nazis created the illusion for them that moving to Terezin was a privilege, relocating to a city in the center of Europe as if it were the "Terezin Spa."*

People went there with visions of a contented lifetime of accommodation, meals, and medical care. One Dutch woman confided to a friend that she had the opportunity to leave her child in the care of a Christian and come alone to Terezin. The Germans falsely told her that the ghetto was very nice, the town was quite large, with playgrounds and gardens, and that it was possible to stay fifteen miles around the town. On the last night before leaving, she decided to take the child with her. "Now she sees and regrets it," an acquaintance of the woman wrote in his diary. Upon arrival in the ghetto, drastic scenes then unfolded. Instead of a spa room, transports were housed in casemates or attics and were given a little coffee substitute with a thin slice of bread for their meals. Many couldn't bear the reality of the situation, and they collapsed mentally and physically. The SS camp commandant, headed by the camp commander, was the master over the life and death of the prisoners. This position was successively held by Dr. Siegfried Seidl, Anton Burger, and Karl Rahm—all of them with the rank of SS-Obersturmfuhrer.

Life in the ghetto was governed by all kinds of orders and prohibitions. The slightest violation was usually followed by severe punishment; the bunkers under the camp commandant's office, where prisoners were interrogated and tortured, were notorious. Two mass executions also took place in the ghetto in early 1942, and prisoners were even hanged for minor offenses such as not greeting an SS officer. Later, punished prisoners were sent to the prison in the Small Fortress, where Jewish prisoners were usually tortured to death. Before the war, the town of Terezin had about 3,500 inhabitants and the same number of soldiers. The Nazis had a goal of placing fifty to sixty thousand Jewish prisoners in the ghetto at one time, which they succeeded in doing after the forced removal of the original inhabitants. In September 1942, more than 58,000 people were crammed into the ghetto. There were only about five square feet per Terezin prisoner. Between fifty and seventy prisoners lived in the barracks rooms, which had previously housed ten soldiers. Thousands of people "lived" in attics without light, without water, without toilets. They endured terrible heat during the summer months and unbearably freezing cold during the winter months. They lived in casemates that were dark and so damp that the army even stopped using them as warehouses.

The food supply and its distribution were disastrous. The food was brought, mostly in barrels or large kettles, to the courtyards of each prisoner barracks. Very hungry prisoners hurried to line up. The healthier, who could run faster, got there first. The older or ill people were served last, and it was mostly cold "food," if there was still something left. Many times, fights broke out; it was literally survival of the still fittest. Therefore, food/bread was the most sought-after commodity for bribing or to obtain some other needed items or favors.

There were also long queues in front of toilets and latrines, and the inhabitants were plagued by bedbugs and rampant epidemics, including typhus. Healthcare was totally inadequate. Between August and October 1942 alone, more than 10,000 prisoners died. In August 1942, Horst Bohme, head of the Protectorate's security police and security service, sent a warning telegram to Berlin that Terezin Ghetto contained more than a tenth of its former inhabitants, and that it was not feasible to send dozens more European Jews there until more barracks could be built. The Berlin organizers of the Final Solution decided on a different resolution: free up the accommodation capacity in the ghetto by implementing more frequent transports to the extermination camps in the East. These transports from Terezin began as early as January 1942. In total, 87,000 prisoners were assigned to them, and only about 3,800 of them lived to see the end of the war.

Of the Terezin transports, more than 83,000 people were killed in the gas chambers or died from hunger, sickness, backbreaking work, or death marches. These were not the only victims; many died within the ghetto. In fewer than four years, 140,000 Jewish prisoners—men, women, and children—passed through Terezin Ghetto. In the last days of the war, they were joined by more than 15,000 members of the evacuation transports that brought Jewish and non-Jewish prisoners from various concentration camps. Of the estimated total of 155,000 men, women, and children who passed through the ghetto, about 35,000 of them found death directly in Terezin, most of them occurring in 1942, numbering as many as 16,000. There were another 83,000 people who perished after deportation from Terezin—in extermination camps, in forced labor camps, and on death marches at the end of the war. Of the 15,000 children who passed through Terezin, 1,086 girls and boys remained in the ghetto in the winter of 1944/45 after the last transport had left. After the end of the war, no more than 142 children over the age of fourteen returned from the concentration camps.

All the passengers, including fourteen-year-old Hana and her family, were directed from the train and the subsequent two-mile walk to the arched passageway of one of the three-story buildings. The square courtyard was soon filled. Myriads of people were looking around, some sitting on the ground trying to recover from their exhaustion; others were physically and emotionally supporting each other, and children's cries were echoing off the walls of the building from various corners. Suddenly, soldiers in black uniforms appeared. They began to divide the women and children to one side and the men to the other in a hurry. The Klein family was separated.

"Don't worry, everything will be all right again!" Hana's father managed to say to her as the SS men pushed him away from the female members of the family.

Hana was in shock. Tears flowed, she felt stifled, gasping for air, she was confused, and she was desperately looking for her father and brother Petr in the opposite crowd. She clenched her grip on her mother, who lovingly patted her and comforted her by telling her that they would all meet again soon. Men in uniforms led the two large groups to different parts of the building.

Hana and her mother soon found themselves in a spacious but modestly-lit basement room. There were several tables against one wall, with women sitting at them. Soldiers with rifles walked behind them. This place was called a "sloijska" in Teutonic jargon. The word comes from the German word "schleuse" or in English "sluice." As new transports arrived in Terezin, they were directed to the basement, frequently to the Hamburg barrack, where they were required to present any personal possessions. Here, they were robbed of some of their last belongings. Practically all new arrivals passed through here, where their registration was carried out. Hana felt uncomfortable in the blizzard of activity, never releasing her spasmodic grip on her mother's hand and surveilling what was going on around her with bulging eyes. She didn't want to get lost here!

Finally, it was their turn. They stood in front of the table, where they had to empty their backpacks and other luggage, and even had to take all the things out of their pockets. They didn't have any valuables on them anymore, but even so, a few articles of her mother's clothes were taken. They were given food vouchers.

Hana could barely stand on her feet anymore. She had had enough for one day; she wanted to crawl somewhere, lie down, and sleep. But suddenly the horrific sight of the pile of corpses at the entrance to the ghetto reappeared in her mind. What did it all mean? What would happen to them next? What now, what tomorrow, the day after tomorrow? Tears welled up in her eyes again. They were taken somewhere again, to another large building not far away. As she later found out, it was one of the former large military barracks.

As soon as they entered, a wretched smell met them. She and her mother had to climb up to the highest, third floor. The large room was filled seemingly to capacity. The Czech gendarmes at the door were giving orders, but Hana could no longer make sense of them. Her mother pulled her by the hand and told her repeatedly that they had to find a place to sleep among the congestion. Most of the bunk beds were already occupied. Some of the prisoners were so fatigued that they organized makeshift beds on the floor, curled up in a ball, using their backpacks as a pillow.

Marta finally found a little free space at the other end of the room on a bunk with mattresses made of straw and covered with coarse burlap. One girl was already lying there, but there was still a little space for the mother and daughter. It was a very modest place, but at least the pair was content for the moment. They didn't hesitate very long to rest, tucking their luggage under the bunk bed and stretching out on the uncomfortable and stinky mattress. As soon as Hana closed her eyes, she succumbed to sleep, despite the murmurs and woeful whimpering that still reigned in the room for a long time afterward.

This was the first night in the Terezin Ghetto. Even in her worst nightmares, she would never guess that she would spend three years there.

Chapter 9

The Podmokel Barracks

Early the next morning, Hana was awakened by an unusual commotion. She sat up on the bunk, watching the human anthill around her. Her mother, meanwhile, had found out where the washrooms were and sent Hana there first. It was a crowded place. And when she peered in through the mass of bodies, she shuddered in disgust, the stench and filth hitting her nose, but it was inescapable. She wanted to leave, but the tidal wave of people pushed her back in. She had no choice. The memory of the glossy bathroom in the family home in Prague's Smichov district had almost faded completely now.

"I must hold on! I have to carry on!" Hana commanded herself, "But can I do it?" Her thoughts also turned to her father and Petr. "Where were they? How were they coping?" she thought.

Breakfast followed (if that's what one could call a small piece of bread and the gray, cloudy liquid her roommates referred to as coffee). They were not allowed out on the street, but at least they could run down to the courtyard, which was surrounded on all sides by the same buildings. Hana and her mother spent one more night in the same room and on the same bunk. When they woke up the next morning, about half of their roommates were no longer there; at that moment they were on a transport to a Nazi camp in the East. Marta and Hana were ordered to move to another barrack. They reassembled their personal belongings and, accompanied by the gendarmes, walked along the road to their new "home"—they were not allowed the privilege of walking on the sidewalk.

They entered a building that bore a striking resemblance to their original Terezin location, Podmokel Barrack. When Hana went inside, her mood improved a little. It seemed that she and her mother were about to experience a possible upgrade in their living conditions: the house was in better condition, and the living rooms were divided by wooden partitions. Even here, though, it was a headache; there were obviously more people living here than would be bearable. The room was No. 60. It was teeming with new residents who were either single women or mothers with their daughters, many around the same age as Hana. There could have been a total of fifty women and children.

There were two-story bunk beds, several tables, and simple benches along the walls. There was a small stove in the corner. They still had to go back downstairs to the gate area, where they were to pick up the remaining suitcases that would be delivered here from the previous barrack, as well as their food vouchers. Outside, Hana saw a group of men standing in front of the house with suitcases in their hands. Her father was among them! She was about to run toward him when her mother firmly stopped her, grabbing her by the arm. Marta made it clear that freedom had its limits here. Women are not allowed to meet men. But after a while, when the patrolling guards moved away, Marta and her daughter threw themselves into Rudolf's arms. It was only for a fleeting moment; they didn't even have time to savor the reunion, but it did instill some sense of hope.

Then they had to go back to their building immediately. A long line began to form in the square courtyard under one of the windows where lunch was being served. When it was Hana and her mother's turn, they each got a scoop of what might have been turnip soup or perhaps a sauce made from unpeeled potatoes, plus a slice of bread, in a tin container. Hana was not able to sleep much the following night. She was overheated. The sweat of the other inmates stagnated in the air, and she could smell human excrement. And then the fleas and bedbugs attacked mercilessly. Hana had previously thought that only dogs had fleas. Now she knew them firsthand. They were intrusive and impossible to get rid of. She could feel them all over her body, biting and sucking blood. When she shooed one away, another one latched on. It was unbearable. The fleas kept coming during the day. Some of the girls competed to see who could catch the most. The pests took up residence in the straw mattresses. And at night, the bedbugs joined in.

"Don't scratch yourself," her mother advised her. But it was hard to stand the nagging and constant sensations on her skin.

To make matters worse, lice gradually joined the ranks. In a few days, they were all covered in them. One night, Hana found a soothing thought in the midst of the misery and smiled at her doll. At least no pests were attacking her! The next day, Marta and Hana received a short message from Rudolf. It was brought by a man who had a pass. On a small note, Rudolf wrote that he and Petr were in a building called Hanover Barrack and that they were fine. He added that he had met his brother, Karl. In an unreal world, it was a small boost, encouraging news. Hana thought that perhaps she might see her father and brother again soon. It was the first time in her life that she hadn't been able to see them in this terrible involuntary separation.

Often her thoughts went back to the carefree times when the whole family was still together. She couldn't understand why all this had happened or why they were in Terezin, a place she had never even heard of before. Her mother was assigned to work in one of the kitchens, fortuitously in the same barrack where they were staying. When Marta told her daughter what she was expected to do each day, Hana was aghast at the demands of her mother's new life and its laborious duties. Marta sat all day with the other women in the circle, peeling potatoes. They sat on low stools. Their backs ached, but neither stretching nor rest was an option. Just scraping and peeling. When some of them needed to relieve themselves, they needed special permission from the supervisor who was looking after them. Hana felt sympathy for her mother. How was she going to manage this? Marta had never done anything like this in her life. But she didn't complain. She tried to maintain some positivity by stroking Hana's cheek or asking her what she had been doing all day. There was no work duty assigned to Hana yet. She didn't even know if she would be assigned anything, and she wasn't allowed to leave the barrack compound. But in the barrack's yard she met other girls her age, where they talked, and at least the time passed more quickly. They talked mostly about their distant home, and about life in freedom. And they wondered what they would do when they got back there.

Table 1. *The Age Composition of the Terezin Prisoners*

	January 1, 1943	December 31, 1943	May 31, 1944
Under 15 years	3,494	3,031	2,722
15 - 60 years	25,036	19,730	18,054
61- 65 years	4,548	3,159	2,240
Over 65 years	16,218	8,735	4,951

Source: *The Final Solution* by Miroslav Karny

One day Hana met a girl named Stella Brollova-Repper. They immediately connected and became great friends, spending every day together when possible. The two girls were the same age. Stella came from the town of Prostejov and arrived in Terezin with her mother, father, and her twin brother. The usual abrupt separation had taken place upon their introduction to Terezin; Stella's father and her brother, Jiri, were moved to a different barrack. Hana and Stella always found a convenient place where they sat close to each other and talked: about school, about their hobbies, but also about food—especially the various treats they liked. That was how they fought off their hunger, or at least that was the goal. They discovered that their families spent similar holidays, going on trips to the countryside and to the mountains. Stella was from an area close to the Jeseniky and Beskydy Mountains. They also got to know other girls, forming groups that walked around the courtyard or hid in more private spaces, so that no one would disturb them. But this facade of passing the days in such an uneventful manner was short-lived.

All children over the age of fourteen had to work in the ghetto. Most of the girls were assigned to work in the Landwirtschaft (agriculture); they were ordered to work in the gardens of Terezin. Waking up early in the morning, all the girls had to line up in the barracks yard. From there, the guard took them to the workplace, which was located in the ditches between the Terezin walls or on the ramparts outside the ghetto. It was June 1942, and the vegetable garden was exhibiting the growth of a variety of plantings. Hana was assigned work next to Stella; they were glad to be outside, and decided it was better than the unkind barracks yard. It was a welcome change. The girls were growing tomatoes, cauliflower, beans, carrots, spinach, celery, parsley, or onions. Apples, cherries, plums, pears, or apricots grew on the fruit trees around the grounds. The girls were led by a master gardener who taught them everything they needed to know. For most of them, including Hana, this was the first manual labor in their lives. Even though it was forbidden, they still managed to occasionally add something flavorful to their monotonous and unpalatable menu. Most of the time they were guarded by Czech gendarmes, but occasionally they managed to smuggle something into the barracks.

Marta Druckerova-Cornell remembered, "When we were assigned to work outside the ghetto, we had to pass by the Czech guards. Mostly there were three of them. We didn't know if they are the good ones or not, especially if they were new guards. But we learned to recognize the good guards very soon. One of the guards was especially good to us. Every time when he was on guard, he concealed for us a large piece of bread with some meat or with a piece of lard. He always put it under one tree in the woods. This act of heroism was very dangerous for him."

The girls hid fruit and vegetables under their clothes, in their bras, in their socks, wherever they could. They took risks under the threat of severe punishment. The produce from the gardens was exclusively for the Nazi guards. Hana worked most often outside the ghetto. Each time they worked, the group of girls had to pass through a barrier where the guards carefully checked the number of girls. A Czech warden was in charge of each work group and guided and monitored the girls as they worked. The gardens were situated along the road to Litomerice, on a hill (ramparts), and the German guards were not very keen to go up there.

But the girls could never be sure when a German guard would appear. And if they did appear, they showed up in the field on horses or bicycles. They behaved like mad dogs, yelling at the girls and sometimes swinging at them with their batons. The girls often smuggled tomatoes or other "goodies" back to the ghetto. The Czech guards warned them before the SS showed up, and they made sure that they weren't stealing anything. If they caught someone stealing, the entire family could be deported with the next transport. Nevertheless, it was worth the risk because the girls were constantly hungry. If they succeeded in bringing some vegetables or fruits back to the barracks, they then shared them with their fellow prisoners or exchanged the goods for a piece of bread. They worked throughout the winter either in the greenhouses or spreading manure in the fields. Sometimes the girls returned to their barracks chilled to the bone, with their fingers aching so much from the cold that they couldn't move them.

Years later, to support this manual labor my mother and others were charged with, I came across a letter from April 1993 written by my mother that was addressed to the Claims Conference in Frankfurt requesting restitution for the tragedies inflicted on her family at the hands of the Nazi regime. Among other accounts, she stated, "In 1944, I also had to tend over 100 pigs, which received much better care and food than we, prisoners."

It took a long time for Hana to get used to the physical work. She worked all day, mostly without much rest. The whole group did not return to their barracks until the evening. Most days after Hana returned, it was not unusual that her mother was still not there. Hana usually attempted to wait for her, but when she couldn't stand the hunger any longer, she ran down to the yard for dinner without her. The evening meal didn't keep her full for long. Occasionally, Marta also managed to sneak something from the kitchen, so she and her daughter shared what little extra they could. They still couldn't see Rudolf or Petr, but they were able to exchange short messages with them occasionally. Notes were brought by prisoners who had special permission. Hana learned that Petr worked as an electrician. She knew her brother had already been interested in various electrical devices at home; he had even built his own radio, of which he was duly proud, but he eventually lost it due to anti-Jewish regulations. Perhaps her father worked as a carpenter building new bunk beds in the quarters? Hana couldn't imagine how he would manage that; he had never done anything like that before. This was true for many people in the ghetto who were forced to learn new skills.

Not long after the transport to Terezin, Hana celebrated her fourteenth birthday on June 21, 1942, but she was not in the mood for a major celebration in this environment. However, she could not help reminiscing on how her parents had always prepared a wonderful festive day for her. And even here in Terezin, her mother did not forget her. Together with Stella and the other girls, she wished her well, and each of them gave Hana at least something small, such as a piece of bread or something else to eat, or even a small bunch of flowers from their confined yard. Hana cried with happiness.

After a few weeks, Stella was reassigned to another job. Apparently helped by her father, she moved to a studio called the "Bauhof"—a construction and craft department, where there were workshops for various crafts such as sculpting, drawing, modeling, and others. (All of the art pieces produced by the prisoners went to the Reich.) By that time, Hana understood very well where she was. What she didn't know, however, was how long she would have to spend there. Each day offered no promises, and learning how to manage life in the ghetto the best she could was all she could focus on. The most challenging trauma she faced was controlling her feelings of fear. It was extremely distressing for her at times. However, she prepared herself for each day, feeling that she was gaining more inner control, more inner strength. It was an exercise in self-preservation.

One evening, Marta told Hana about her parents, Hana's grandparents: Hermina and Rudolf. Hana had asked about them before the family left for Terezin, but neither of her parents had told her anything . . . until now. Hana loved her grandparents very much, and she often went to the village of Letky near Prague to visit them with the whole family before the occupation. And she always looked forward to going there, because her grandmother was a good cook and made fantastic cakes. Her mother now revealed to her that her grandmother and grandfather had already been included in one of the first transports to Lodz, Poland, in the autumn of 1941. But she refrained from sharing their fate with her daughter; they had been killed there by the Nazis. Marta also told her that she had met a young lady in the kitchen named Hilda Taussigova, who was from Zabreh in Moravia.

"She is fifteen years younger than me, but we get along very well," she confided to her daughter.

Unbeknownst to Hana at that moment, Hilda would later become a guardian angel for her, helping her through difficult times in her life. However, she did not even hear the rest of her mother's story, because she fell asleep from fatigue.

Any dream she could have would be better than the nightmare she was living.

Chapter 10

Island in Hell

In the autumn of 1942, the first major turning point came in Hana's life in the ghetto. She had to be separated from her mother and was assigned to building L410, a newly established girls' housing, while her mother stayed in the previous barracks in the kitchen. It was in L410 that Hana spent most of her Terezin imprisonment. It still stands in Terezin today in the square next to the church. The ground floor houses the municipal police, with two more floors above it with apartments. In the times of the ghetto, these were quarters for young Jewish women prisoners.

"On the ground floor, there was a small office, a bread dispenser, and something like a tailor's shop for the home. The rooms in which the girls lived were a little larger. In the basement was the schoolroom, a vast room with desks for the children. The windows were just little air holes at street level," one of the girls who lived to see the liberation described the building years later.

On average, about 350 girls lived in the building, but the occupancy changed constantly as transports of new residents arrived in the ghetto, and others left for Auschwitz and other camps in the East. The transport from Terezin was a constant threat. None of the camp's inhabitants knew what the next day would bring. Who would stay? Who would leave? From one day to the next, the girls' roommates, often their best friends, disappeared.

"After the autumn transports, we returned to our room one evening and didn't know what to do. Almost all the girls and the governesses were gone. The mood in the ghetto was fearful. Many windows were open, many rooms were completely empty," Vera Bendova-Gulikova, a roommate, described the atmosphere there after a series of transports to Auschwitz.

Hana was assigned to Room 29, on the highest floor in the corner. As in the other quarters, there were several rows of three-story bunk beds with rough mattresses filled with straw. Girls aged twelve to sixteen, some probably a little older, lived throughout the house. The older girls, including Hana, went to work in the gardens. The Jewish leaders were in charge of the living quarters and the individual rooms, and great emphasis was placed on cleanliness; every day the floor had to be dusted, swept, and mopped. The dishes were washed under the pump. In the evenings, Hana studied, but there were also various musical performances or lectures. These offerings were all part of the propaganda machine of the Nazis and a characteristic that made Terezin unique from other concentration camps and ghettos.

Because of the strict regime and the endless uncertainty of the future, many girls spoke of L410 as an island in hell. However, many strong friendships and bonds were formed here, with girls helping each other and giving each other small gifts for birthdays or other holidays, anything to distract themselves from the reality they were living. They relied on each other for any kind of emotional support to help them survive.

The Sixth Historical Stop

Working for the Reich

The Germans were losing the war. Nazi successes on the fronts turned into failures. There was growing pressure in Germany and the occupied states to increase war munitions and accoutrements. Prisoners, including those in the Terezin Ghetto, were not to be left behind in this effort and were expected to produce materials such as uniforms, winter clothes, etc., for the army. By December 1943, more than sixty percent of the prisoners were already in the labor force. The problem, however, was that about 90% of the ghetto's working capacity was used for its own operations, even though according to the then-applicable guidelines for concentration camps, no more than one-tenth of the prisoners could be released for internal use. In Terezin, the ratio was in direct contrast, and the ghetto command probably adjusted the figure even further. Thus, work for the Reich was not very significant during the entire period of the Terezin Ghetto's operation. For example, stockings for the Wehrmacht and the riot police were repaired by a group of female prisoners from April to June 1942, using leftover scrap material from unrepairable stockings. This was followed by the sewing of uniforms, but this was a one-off affair from June to September 1942.

The two most important production programs thus became those described in Nazi documents as "war important." The first was the so-called "Production K," for which a large circus-style tent was erected on the square in Terezin, with two smaller tents attached as warehouses. "In reality, it was not a place of production but used for the packing of winter equipment for motor vehicles into 120,000 boxes. The parts were sent to Terezin from various places in Germany and the occupied territories. Also, the boxes were just assembled in the camp," from the book The Final Solution. The problem was that there were enough boxes, but not enough material to fill them. One of the female prisoners described how the Terezin commandant's office dealt with this. In total, a thousand prisoners were deployed for this work, supervised by Czech gendarmes and SS officers. The last box was packed and shipped in November 1943, after which the large tent was torn down. Most of the Production K prisoners were subsequently included in the December transports to Auschwitz. An important wartime production program was the splitting of mica, the thin slices of which were used as insulation in the manufacture of aircraft. Work began in June 1942 and continued until early 1945. However, production did not run continuously and was suspended at the end of 1943 and only resumed in early September 1944.

On average, nearly 850 women worked in the mica plant, and they were given 6,288 kilograms of material to process, of which they chipped 2,226 kilograms of mica, or approximately one third. This was justified by the poor quality of the material supplied. Other production programs and work activities also included the manufacture of ink powder, spraying uniforms with white covering paint, sewing one part of a parachute, making boxes for cartridges, making handbags or lampshades, toys, or decorative metal goods. The intent of the SS was partly to demonstrate their active approach to war production and, partly, the production was for the personal use of the ghetto commanders.

I managed to track down and interview dozens of women and their relatives, many decades later, who lived in building L410 and even some who lived in Room 29 with my mother. "In Room 29, I shared a bunk with Eva Steinova-Klinger. Hanka slept in the third top bunk together with Ilona Steinova-Weinstock, and they were great friends," Fanda Neubauerova-Nassau confided to me when I visited her at her home in California. She recalled that about twenty-five girls slept in the room—sometimes a little more, sometimes fewer, depending on how the transports arrived with new prisoners or how the trains to the killing camps left on the other side. "There was only one toilet and one sink on the whole floor for all of us. Every morning, there was a long line of girls from all the rooms standing in front of the toilet. I remember Hana very well. She was a very beautiful girl with fine long black hair," stated Fanda.

In the evenings, the girls studied, sang songs, or played games. Hana was duly proud of her dark hair, but then something happened that was hard for her to cope with. Stella Brollova-Repper, whom I visited several times in Virginia, recalled that all the occupants of Room 29, and, in fact, the entire L410 building, were livid. "So, there was a regulation that we [our hair] had to be cut short. Suddenly we looked like boys, and we couldn't recognize each other. We all got over it, but our Hana didn't. It broke Hanka's heart," recalled Stella. "Our room guardian or 'Betreuerka' [supervisor] and teacher was Rosa Schulhof. She was a professor; she taught history, and she approached the heartbroken Hanka and told her, 'Don't worry, your hair will grow long again soon.' And so it was, and her beautiful black hair was soon back to its full glory. And ours, too."

According to Stella, Hana brought several nice pieces of clothing to the ghetto: skirts and blouses. "But maybe she got them in Terezin, I do not remember anymore. She [Hana] always wanted to dress nicely. Even for work in the gardens. She had a blue and white checked skirt that I liked very much. I was the same size as Hanka, so I often borrowed that skirt from her. I just wanted to wear something different," said Stella.

Rosa Schulhofova was very keen on education. It was no wonder she spent many long hours educating her pupils of Room 29, reading Czech history to them in the evenings, or having them draw and play games with her. But she was also a great stickler for personal hygiene and cleanliness; every morning, she designated two girls to clean the room. Vera Bendova-Gulikova and Anna Lorencova recall that Rosa was a communist before the war and tried to transmit this ideology to the girls. "It was hard to resist when you didn't know anything about it. The theory itself was beautiful. But Hanka Kleinova and some of the other girls could not be influenced; they were not up to it," both women agreed. Stella Brollova-Repper also recalled how sometimes the girls slept on the floor, in the corridors, or even outside in the yard. "It wasn't allowed, but the number of fleas and bedbugs in our bed was unbearable; it was impossible to sleep," Stella said.

In addition, their daily challenges included a lack of quality food, insufficient hygiene (most of the toilets were not flushable, and water often did not flow), as well as the expected physical and mental exhaustion. The girls were also plagued by various epidemic diseases, including hepatitis and measles. Many people did not survive the diseases. "But Hanka was never sick. She was probably the only one of us. She was a really unusual exception," remarked Stella. "Her dad would come to see her regularly, giving her, I think, some medicine. I don't know what it was, but it's quite possible that it saved Hanka's life. He probably had some good contacts in the ghetto and probably on the outside of the ghetto, because these medicines must have been smuggled in," offered Stella. She remembered that Hana's father used to come to Hana early in the mornings before the girls went to work in the gardens. "He came when an epidemic started, which happened very often." But her father used to come to see Hana even when there was no epidemic. She loved her father very much. He wanted to see her, wanted to know she was all right. Sometimes he'd bring her a bit of food.

According to Stella, Hana was often visited by her brother Petr as well. When possible, which was not too often, they used to walk around the ghetto together or just sit on the lower bunk bed in the room and talk. These were very special occasions. "But I never saw Hanka's mother," added Stella. Marta Druckerova-Cornell, who also lived in Room 29, knew Hana's mother. "She worked in the same kitchen with my sister. It was very hard work. They peeled the stinking potatoes and then cooked them in sauce. Once a week, there was also something like dumplings to eat," Druckerova-Cornell remembered. "In the morning, they served black water, which was called coffee, and in the evening the same thing. Sometimes we children were given a snack, dirty potato water, a piece of bread, margarine, and a little sugar. Most of us ate it right away. We poured the sugar in our mouths [and] added margarine. We would have to wait again for a whole week for the next ration. Sometimes Hanka, some of the other girls as well, and I stole something in the gardens and secretly brought it to the room, where we always shared the prize. But it was very dangerous. When someone was caught, the whole family got on a transport to the East." Marta recalled that she and Hana were not the best of friends, but they got along well. "Hanka was younger, and she was mostly friends with Ilona Steinova, Stella Brollova, and also with Vera Lustig, who didn't return from Auschwitz," Marta said.

Marta noted that they didn't have much free time, because most of the day was taken up with work in the gardens. They worked even in freezing weather. "The Germans always invented work. For example, we painted the frames of the greenhouse windows. We hoed the edges of the beds. We were outside all day; it was very cold." The threat of being transported to Auschwitz or another camp in the East was always hovering over the ghetto inhabitants. "Those transports were scary for us children and sad for many. No one knew if or when they would be called. Families were separated, and at the trains, parents and children often saw each other for the last time in their lives. Some children didn't even know that someone close to them had gone. Maybe it was even better that way. Only people from the new transports that arrived in Terezin Ghetto or from the more willing Czech gendarmes provided connections with the outside world," Marta recalled.

In the evenings, sometimes the light did not work because the electricity was turned off, so the girls lay on the bunk beds in the dark. "Each of us had a story to tell," Marta told me. "For example, I made up that my daddy's name was Spytihnev, and we children called him Spito and my mother Hnevo. I don't even know how I came up with that." Or a circle of girls would form, and Marta would teach them rhyming dirty poems. "We had a great laugh!" The girls also often talked about food because they were all hungry.

Maud Stecklmacherova-Beer, who moved to Israel after the war, also remembered Hana. She worked with her in the Terezin gardens. "Hanicka was really a very nice young girl. She was friendly, kind, and helpful. We all liked her. Even today, I remember her very well," Maud remembered years later. She also spoke of working in the garden as extremely challenging. "We were still glad to get out, even though we were hungry, and the work was hard all day. We worked until late autumn, often in winter too. We were supervised by Czech gendarmes; sometimes they brought us hot soup, which was very dangerous for them. But we were extremely grateful to them."

For Hana, there was some small comfort in knowing she was not alone.

Chapter 11

The Bartered Bride

I remember when I was a little boy, we shared a little cultural experience in our family. How nice it was to see *The Bartered Bride*, the famous comic opera by the well-known composer Bedrich Smetana, on television. We were snuggled up in bed: my father Jarek on one side, my mother Hana on the other, and me in the middle between them. My two younger brothers were already asleep in the next room. Later, when I too had children of my own, my daughter Hana and her grandmother Hana went to see *The Bartered Bride* (also known as *The Sold Bride*) at the National Theatre in Prague at least twice. In researching my mother's past, I realized why she loved the production so much, and why I had seen the opera with her perhaps ten times. It was most likely one of her most pleasant memories of Terezin, although she never told me, of course. I didn't realize this until after her death. *The Bartered Bride* was one of the many musical works staged in Terezin by prisoners.

Culture and art in such a place were a refreshing diversion from the daily barrage of orders and regulations and strict rules from early morning until evening. It temporarily muffled the permanent hunger, fear for loved ones and themselves, and questions about who would be included on the next transport to the East. Consequently, concerts of all arts, theatrical performances, and other cultural activities were moments of relative happiness in the midst of evil. As mother's prisoner friend Ela Steinova-Weissberger told me during our visit in Terezin, "Nobody can imagine what it meant for us visiting cultural activities." She continued, "While there, we could suppress, for a while, the constant fear and daily struggle to survive. We even felt moments of happiness."

Hana was involved in some cultural activities with her friends. Although she was not an excellent singer, she went to various musical performances and other shows when she could. She sat and listened, feeling the tones within her whole body, and she found her thoughts escaping from the misery of Terezin to other heavenly realms. All she had to do was close her eyes, listen, forget about the present, and let herself drift without worry.

My mother Hana was particularly fond of the conductor Karel Ancerl, of whom she later often spoke, avoiding mention of Terezin.

Ancerl, together with his wife and parents, was deported to Terezin in the autumn of 1942 and founded an improvised string orchestra in the ghetto. Hana attended some of his concerts. Ancerl's wife gave birth to a son, Jan, in Terezin in 1943, but a year later the whole family, including the parents, were transported to Auschwitz. Ancerl's wife, parents, and the young son were killed there. He was liberated in the Friedland labor camp, from where he walked back to Terezin in search of his surviving relatives. He found only his maternal uncle and his older son. In 1950, he became the director of the Czech National Philharmonic. In 1968, he emigrated to Toronto. My mother loved his concerts. It wasn't until much later that I realized—as with *The Bartered Bride*—how personal it was for her.

When the children's opera *Brundibar*, written between 1938 and 1939 by Hans Krasa and Adolf Hoffmeister, was performed in Terezin, it was an immensely meaningful experience for Hana, all the other children, as well as the adults in the ghetto. The librettist, Adolf Hoffmeister, unlike Hans Krasa, the composer, managed to protect himself from the German occupiers by emigrating to England. "In essence, we conceived the opera as a Brechtian play bringing an illuminating lesson," said Ela Steinova-Weissberger.

Brundibar is a simple fairy tale-like story. The mother is ill and her two children, Joe (Pepi) and Annette (Aninka), go to get milk for her, but they have no money. That's when they see passers-by giving money to the organ-grinder named Brundibar. So, they stand on the corner and start singing in hopes of earning some money. But their voices are too weak, and Brundibar tries to chase them away. Then various animals from the town come and advise them to form a children's choir to make their voices sound stronger. The animals invite a few more schoolchildren, and the children start singing in strong voices. Brundibar is chased away and defeated. The perseverance and the solidarity of the children resulted in triumph over the organ-grinder because they did not give up.

Hana watched the incredibly spontaneous performance of the children. Their production spilled over into the audience as if at that moment the entire hall had transcended Terezin to the free world. There was nothing of the evil world during the performance. The children played for their lives. For all of them, Brundibar was the embodiment of evil, of their misfortune, of Hitler. The final applause was incredible. A sense of accomplishment ran through the bodies of all the child actors.

"Every time we sang the final 'Brundibar defeated' at the end, there was thunderous applause, and the audience wanted to hear the song again and again, until they almost had to throw us out. We all enjoyed that moment of freedom," Ela Steinova-Weissberger, who played the role of the Cat during all 55 performances, recalled after the war.

"And then there was something else," Ela added. "We had to visibly wear a yellow Star of David on our clothes. Only when we played Brundibar did we not have to have it. That was the only exception. For that moment, we were not marked with a Jewish star, and that meant we were free for that moment. But the biggest star was the organ-grinder Brundibar, played by Jan Treichlinger. Every time Hanka met him, she called out to him, 'Brundibar, Brundibar!' Other ghetto residents reacted the same way. They all liked him very much. Even though he played a bad man who didn't like children, he performed the role of the organ player in such a way that he won universal admiration and appreciation. He was simply amazing!" Ela concluded. The audience later remembered the little actor. Unfortunately, he was later deported to Auschwitz and was killed in one of the gas chambers. Performances like this one were prohibited by the ghetto rulers.

However, as Ela remembered, "We always worried whether the Nazis would really let us put on the opera. Sometimes the guards seemed to look the other way and allowed prisoners to perform concerts and plays at the end of the day. The Nazis may have known about the opera but chose not to interfere. They were anticipating that we would all be killed soon anyway."

<u>*The Seventh Historical Stop*</u>

In Terezin, the Muses Did Not Keep Silent

The most famous cultural performance in Terezin Ghetto was undoubtedly the children's opera Brundibar, which was staged by the Czech-German-Jewish composer Hans Krasa in collaboration with Frantisek Zelenka. It premiered in September 1943 and was performed more than fifty times. There was avid interest among the prisoners. Krasa did not see his liberation, and in October 1944, he was included in one of the last transports to Auschwitz. Although he was not yet forty-five years old, he was immediately sent to the gas chamber as an "older man" on the infamous Auschwitz ramp, where life and death decisions were made after the arrival of the transports. There was, however, another Krasa who lived in Terezin and made his mark on the history of artistic activity there. His name was Edgar, but he was called Eda. He sang in the Terezin choir. He survived, and at the end of the war, he managed to escape from the death march.

Eda was born in 1924 to a Jewish family in Karlovy Vary. Nine years later, the family moved to Prague, where Eda trained as a cook in the popular restaurant U Rozvarilu. In the autumn of 1941, he left with the first transport to the Terezin Ghetto, where he continued to work as a cook. "We arrived at the Sudeten Barracks, the gates closed, and the 'Lagerkommandant' (Commandant of the ghetto) recited all the prohibitions to us. There was very little left to do. Only then did I realize that we were prisoners," *he later recalled in* Rosh Chodesh *magazine.*

In Terezin, Eda subsequently met the conductor and composer Rafael Schachter, who had played with E. F. Burian, conducted choirs, and taught piano. One of Schachter's most famous achievements was the staging of Verdi's Requiem *with Terezin prisoners, which included Eda Krasa. But the prisoners also sang* The Bartered Bride, The Marriage of Figaro, The Mouthpiece, *and* The Magic Flute. *According to Krasa, Schachter tried to stage Verdi to convey an indirect message to the ghetto Nazis:* "When the Supreme Judge judges, no sinner will escape." *The Requiem premiered in January 1944, and in June 1944, there was one performance for high-ranking SS officers and members of the International Committee of the Red Cross who were in Terezin for an inspection. There were fifteen performances in all, and Schachter died in January 1945 on the death march from Auschwitz. Krasa was deported to the*

Auschwitz extermination camp in September 1944, and then went further on to Gleiwitz, a sub-camp of Auschwitz, where he repaired wagons.

In January 1945, he managed to escape from the death march and returned to Prague. He was happily reunited with his parents, married in November 1949, and a year later, he and his wife managed to get to Israel after several attempts. There he worked as a chef and later worked in the management of restaurants and hotels. He also taught future chefs to assist as part of Israeli aid to African countries. In the 1960s, he moved to the United States, settling in Boston, where he owned a restaurant. He died in February 2017 at the age of 93.

The story of Eda Krasa demonstrates how cultural life in the Terezin Ghetto developed to an extraordinary degree. Among the tens of thousands of prisoners who passed through, many were not only distinguished professional artists, but also enthusiastic amateurs. Only a few lived to see liberation. At first, the SS commandant merely tolerated their activities; later, in connection with the use of the Terezin Ghetto for propaganda purposes, the Jewish authorities were allowed considerable latitude in this area. Thus, a department for the organization of leisure time (Freizeitgestaltung) could be established, which organized a whole range of cultural activities. Significant works of art were produced in Terezin, and purely entertaining artistic genres, including cabarets and revues, were also practiced. The common feature of all the activities, however, was the strengthening of one's own spirit and that of one's fellow prisoners, and the fostering of optimism and faith in a better future. Many of the cultural activities had a clear symbolic meaning—they expressed resistance to the German occupiers and, more pointedly, to Adolf Hitler.

Many children and adolescents were involved in cultural life. "Their work was characterized by an unusual maturity and was proof, among other things, that children and young people in conditions of imprisonment were rapidly growing older and soon saw the world through the eyes of their adult fellow prisoners" (Holocaust.cz). A typical example is the magazine Vedem (translated as "We Lead" or "Leader"). This was a self-created work by young writers, including the poet Hanus Hachenburg, who only lived to be fifteen years old. The magazine's central figure was Petr Ginz, who was transported from Prague to Terezin in the autumn of 1942 when he was fourteen. He loved literature, especially the novels of Jules Verne, and then began to write his own short stories, culminating in a novel that he illustrated himself. Shortly after his arrival in the ghetto, he and other teen boys began to publish Vedem, for which he edited and wrote articles, poems or painted illustrations. In September 1944, he was assigned to a transport to Auschwitz, where he was killed.

On January 16, 2003, the first Israeli astronaut, Ilan Ramon, flew into space aboard the American space shuttle Columbia. He took with him a copy of Petr's 1942 drawing "Lunar Landscape." Returning from its space mission, the shuttle burned up on reentry into the Earth's atmosphere. There were no survivors among the crew. The tragedy took place on February 1, 2003—Petr Ginz's birthday.

Hana, too, considered an artistic career. In Terezin, she became friends with the writer and journalist Norbert Fryd, who persuaded her to apply to the music conservatory in Prague when the war was over. I don't know why my mother never pursued it; perhaps she was not convinced of her talent. But if she lacked the ability, undoubtedly, she would not have received such an offer.

Norbert Fryd suffered many tragedies. In 1939, at the age of 26, after graduating from law school, he was expelled for racial reasons from the Prague Faculty of Philosophy, where he was studying literature. He was subsequently deported to Terezin Ghetto and Auschwitz and lived to see the end of the war in the Kaufering concentration camp in Germany. His parents, brother and wife, and their child, who was less than a year old, were murdered. At the end of his 1971 book, *Bottled Mail*, I read his life confession and about his experience of the occupation: "I will return to Prague soon and go to the faculty to get my long-overdue diploma. There will be a graduation. When it comes to thanking my parents, I will take a step forward and point to the empty seats. They were reserved for my mother, for my father, for my brother and one for Helen with the baby in her arms. Then I explain everything to my friends in the auditorium: what happened to my people, [and] why I'm standing here so late and alone."

He was not alone in that experience.

Chapter 12

The Counting of
Bohusovice Basin

The 11th of November 1943 was a cold and rainy day. When Hana got up before five in the morning, she had not had a restful night, not unlike many of the girls in the room. There was something in the air. It was an uneasy feeling. When she returned to her quarters in Room 29 later that evening, would all her friends still be there? Or would she never see some of them again? And what would happen to her? Would she come back? Would she even live to see this evening? She shivered partly from the dampness and partly from fear. The uncertainty was cruelly daunting and the most horrible feeling, day in and day out. It made some people insane. She could tell from the other girls' expressions that she was not the only one feeling this way.

What was the source of the disquietude? The previous day, an order was given announcing that the following day, all the inhabitants must move to the nearby Bohusovice Basin, where a census of ALL from the ghetto would take place. Bohusovice Basin or Hollow (as stated in some publications) was a large open area just outside the Terezin ramparts accessible by the south-east gate. It was surrounded by a low ridge. When about 30,000 prisoners were held there, they were guarded by many Nazi soldiers with machine guns and dogs standing on the ridge. Escaping was impossible.

These gatherings and roll calls seemed endless and were often cruelly and unnecessarily extended as disciplinary exercises to make all of the prisoners suffer the long wait (which could be hours). This time it was prompted by the Nazi headquarters' arrest of deputy Jewish elder Jakob Edelstein and several other people from the central registry. They were accused of falsifying the records of prisoners who were designated to be transported to the East. It was viewed as an intentional attempt to cover up the escapes from the ghetto and the discovery that some prisoners had not boarded transports bound for the designated camps. There were about five or ten suspects identified.

Hana knew Jakob Edelstein, having met him several times on the streets of the ghetto. An older fellow inmate told her how Edelstein, before being transported to Terezin, tried to advise his fellow Jews to travel to Palestine or other safe countries—until the German

authorities stopped the emigration. Edelstein's attention eventually turned to the Terezin prisoners, and he was among the first
to arrive in the ghetto in December 1941. He was appointed to the
local Jewish self-government, which he headed until January 1943,
when he became deputy Jewish "commander." He tried to negotiate
what he could for the ghetto inhabitants. "He intervened without
humility, openly and manfully, with a direct look in the eyes; he
did not slouch, he stood morally and mentally above them! Even the
officers felt it—they were afraid of Edelstein. He was a modern hero,
the most modern of the oldest Jews, young and smiling, kind and
good both to his grandmother, who had her life behind her, and to
the child playing in the dust of a backstreet in the ghetto among the
carcasses of rats and the remains of the previous day's hailstorm . . ."
Czechoslovakian Jewish writer and journalist Frantisek Robert Kraus
wrote of him after the war.

When Hana walked down the stairs at 5 a.m. on November 11,
1943, toward the courtyard where the girls from the entire barrack
of L410 were to gather, she already knew that Edelstein had been
arrested. The news had spread very fast around the ghetto the
previous day. The camp whisper was efficient. But she did not know
what happened to Edelstein next. He was transported to Auschwitz,
as were his wife Miriam and his twelve-year-old son Ariem, and they
were all executed on June 20, 1944, in Auschwitz. The Nazis allegedly killed Edelstein's wife and child first in front of him and then
executed him.

Hana stood among the other girls that morning, wearing the
warmest clothes she had. And she carried for the day with her three
ounces of sugar, one pound of bread, or a piece of pâté. The girls tried
to convince themselves that nothing was out of the ordinary. It was
just a one-day exercise, and then they would all soon return to their
rooms again. But even so, the nervousness could not be completely
quelled, and they talked quietly, trying to suppress their anxiety. Was
this really just a simple count? Was it just an excuse for something
worse? Could something happen to us? We were supposed to take
food with us, so doesn't that mean we're going to get a ride somewhere? Somewhere far away? The girls stood in the courtyard for

an hour, but the command came to tell them to go back to their rooms. We were not going anywhere after all? Some of the girls were relieved by the news, but about ten minutes later, the shrill whistle of one of the guards could be heard again, calling the entire house of about 350 girls back to the yard.

The whole procession started to march. There were tens of thousands of prisoners from all over the ghetto, and they were on the move. Infants were being carried in the arms of their parents or pushed in a makeshift stroller, and small, fearful children were clinging convulsively to their mothers' hands. There were all ages of adult men and women, including invalids practically crawling with crutches or being supported by their relatives and acquaintances. Only the very ill who were near death and ailing in the barracks didn't go. Many prisoners were visibly panic-stricken, fearing the worst, while others appeared calm, trying to reassure those around them. The slow-moving and long lines of apprehensive prisoners were accompanied by the guards, who constantly barked at anyone who could not keep up with the pace of the majority.

The girls from Room 29 arrived in the Bohusovice Basin before long. Endless hours of standing in one place awaited them. Hours of uncertainty and fear. All were cramped tightly together. "We were together with the children," one of the L410 guardians later recalled. "And we invented different games to occupy the youngsters: word games, riddles, the kind of games you play with children when you have nothing else at hand, just to distract the children so they don't get scared. We were afraid of being shot ourselves. We didn't know if we would come back."

Hana, like the other prisoners in the basin, grew very cold. Her hands and feet were freezing. She shivered not only from the cold, but also from a fear that could not be smothered. Armed SS and gendarmes stood around the entire basin. At one point, a whisper began to spread through the crowd that everyone in the basin would be shot. Hana's adrenaline surged, and tears appeared. She trembled even more. Are we really all going to die here? Some of the older prisoners remembered the beginning of 1942, when two mass executions took place in the ghetto. At that time, the death sentences were for prisoners who had not committed any serious offenses: those who had sent messages from Terezin or those who had not saluted an SS officer. They were hanged.

Hana tried to find her mother, father, and brother, but she was unable to do so among tens of thousands of people, and nobody could leave the place where they were standing. The other girls who wanted to be with their loved ones before they died were thinking the same. "We really thought we would never come back. On a higher ground around the basin, the Nazis placed several automatic machine gun[s]," one of Hana's friends told me after the war.

The wait was endless. Hana's legs ached. One woman spread a blanket on the cold, damp ground, on which she sat with her two small children, and told them stories. It was almost unbelievable, but she even managed to make them laugh. When Hana heard the children's spontaneous laughter, it sounded like a voice of hope. More waiting. Nature took its course. When one of the girls needed to use the bathroom, her friends formed a circle around her for privacy.

Suddenly, a sharp command rang through the valley, "Get in centennials!" (rows of ten). There was an organized bustle among the prisoners. Anton Burger, the camp commander, rode in on horseback from Terezin, planes circled in the sky, dogs barked, SS men rode by on bicycles, and other guards had their weapons ready. Assembled prisoners heard the gunshots, which were not too distant, and only increased the general nervousness. What will happen to us? Hana looked around in alarm. She saw several women taking their small children in their arms and embracing them more tightly. It was as if they were expecting the end.

But nothing happened. They were still alive!

The day was already slowly turning into night. The sun was setting; the shadows were getting longer; the darkness was getting darker. The old and unwell people were struggling to remain standing and finally began sinking to the ground. Hana also saw several people who had fainted, and their friends were trying to help them. The stench of human excrement was unbearable.

The very ill remained in the ghetto on sick leave. The hospital in Terezin was so full that some beds were occupied by two people, while for others there was no room, so they spent the whole day sitting up. Martha Frohlich, who lived in the room next to Hana's, was among the sick with a high fever. "I was sick from morning until evening, lying on the bed, unable even to go to the toilet. I was forced to leave anyway, making room for older severely ill persons," she noted in her recollection after the war. "And they kept counting us like cattle, over and over again. I heard planes and also shots; I thought they were going to shoot us all."

And then something unimaginable happened. A loud order was heard in Czech, "Back to the ghetto!" Hana thought at that moment that a miracle had happened. Some of the girls cried after the endless suspense and then the unexpected sudden relief. They all slowly made their way back to their quarters. They hated the ghetto, but hell on earth suddenly turned into paradise on earth. The surviving Terezin magazine *Vedem* described the scene:

> A great movement. Like when a rope is loosened and everything snaps. We walked forward. Who gave the command is not known, but it went. Like a slow-moving avalanche that kills. A squeeze. You could hear the screams. There was reckless trampling. Everybody is thinking of themselves. Me, no one else! It was a matter of life. We made it to the barracks that blocked our way. The whole mass compressed into one mass. You couldn't breathe and everything stood still. Everyone was drifting, almost unaware of themselves. The strength of the individual was not valid, the cordons holding the organization were pushed back. Only one terrible force was exerted, and that was the force of the whole, unstoppable and cruel. Yes, and yet we got home. No one knows exactly how. Everyone fled, leaving everything behind. We came out of it like a fly out of a spider's web, with a look of astonishment on our faces, but accustomed to such things.

When Hana and the other girls returned to Room 29, the small stove was already hot and spreading an unexpected comforting warmth. Hana climbed up to her top bunk and fell asleep immediately. She didn't even have the strength to take off her clothes after her interminable physical and mental exhaustion.

Two days later, on November 13th, the daily order of the Jewish Self-government No. 37 was published. It stated, "The management and the Council of Elders thank all the inhabitants of the ghetto, especially the building management authorities, the guards, the ghetto and economic department, the medical and other nursing staff, the staff of the central registry, as well as the work groups who helped in the entry and exit process, for the discipline which they all exhibited by the census carried out in the Bohusovice Basin on November 11, 1943."

Like flies escaping a spider's web, we displayed an initial look of astonishment on our faces, but sadly became accustomed to such events.

Chapter 13

Photos

1994: Hana Kleinova Fristensky

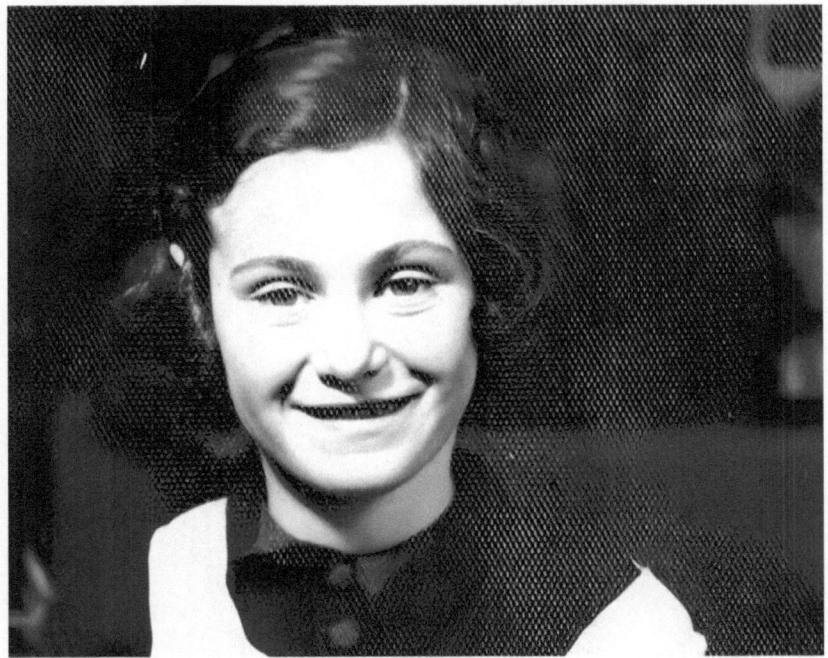

1937: Hana Kleinova

1936: Hana with her father, Rudolf, in Karlovy Vary.

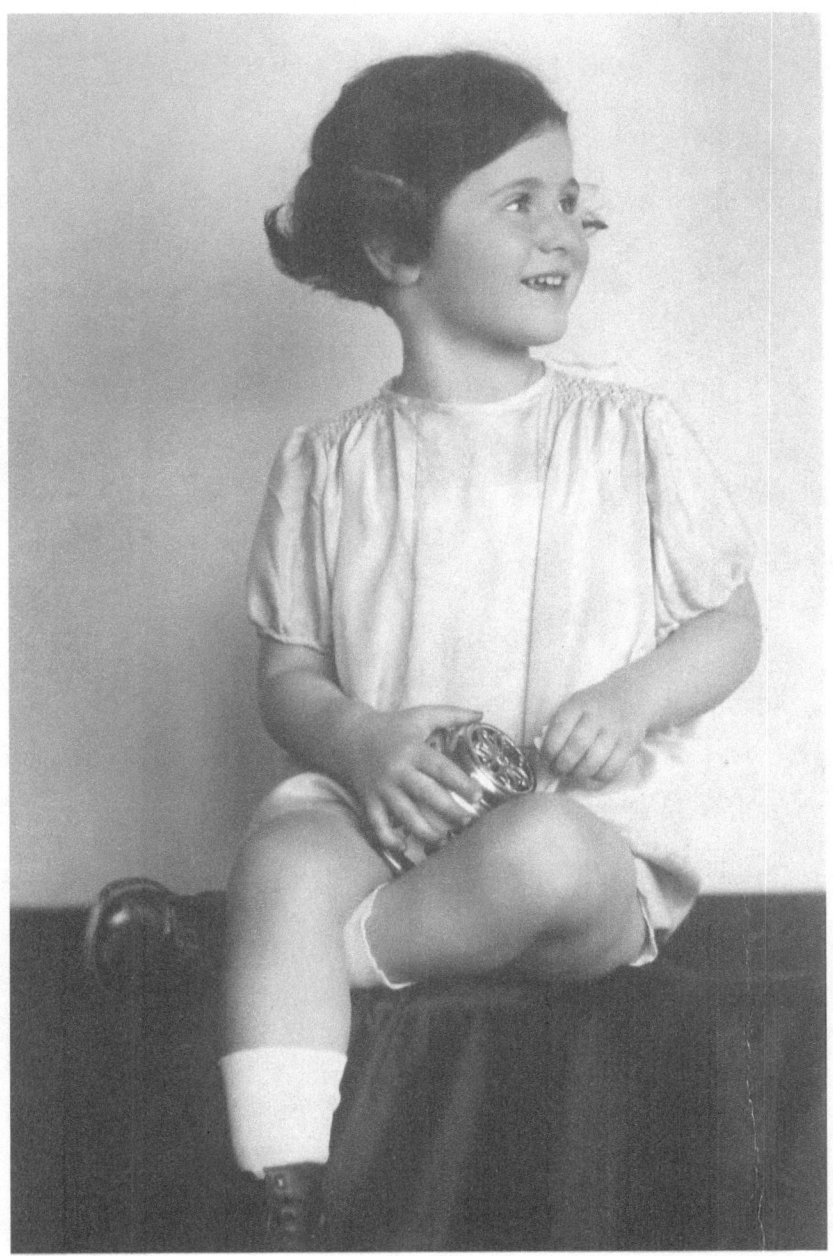

1931: Hana Kleinova, three years old.

1931: Hana Kleinova at home in Prague-Smichov.

1932: Hana at Kramarova hut in the mountains with Petr and the doll that she took with her to Terezin Ghetto.

1935: Petr and Hana Klein.

1935: The Klein family in Prague.

1936: The Klein family in the White Mountain (Krkonose), Czechoslovakia - Rudolf, Hana, Petr, Marta.

1938: Hana in school photo.

1944: Hana featured in the Nazi propaganda movie working in the Terezin garden.

1947: Hana and Petr in Prague.

1947: Hana in Zabreh.

1947: Hana Kleinova and Jaromir Fristensky at the Morava River.

1947: Hilda Taussigova Sladka and Hana Kleinova in Zabreh in Moravia.

1947: Hana posing at a castle ruin in Moravia.

1948: Hana Kleinova and Jaromir Fristensky, wedding photo.

1949: Hana with firstborn son, Frantisek, in Stromovka Park, Prague.

1949: Hana (center) as a team handball member in Bedihost.

1911: The Fristensky brothers - Frantisek, Josef, Karel, and Gustav, professional wrestlers

1949: Marie and Frantisek Fristensky welcoming their first grandson, Frantisek, at their family farm in Bedihost.

1951: Jaromir and Hana Kleinova Fristensky with their son, Frantisek.

1983: Hana and Stella Brollova-Repper in Switzerland
(roommates from Terezin Ghetto).

1984: The last photo together of Hana and Petr, with their cousin Irena in Zurich.

1985 With Arnost Lustig at American University, Washington, DC.

1988: Hana vacationing with granddaughter, Hana, in France.

1996: Frank with mother Hana in Feldkirch, Austria.

1995: Former roommates in Terezin ghetto from Room #29 - Hana Kleinova-Fristensky, Alena Synkova-Munkova, Eva Steinova-Klingerova, and Martha Druckerova-Cornell.

1996: Misha, Nadia, Victoria Butler-Fristensky, Hana, and Hana Kleinova-Fristensky in Taos Pueblo, NM.

2015: Frank with Ela Steinova -Weissberger in Tappan, NY.

2015: Frank with Stella Brollova-Repper in Falls Church, VA.

2016: Frank with Ilona Steinova -Weinstock in Los Angeles, CA.

2017: Frank and family - Hana, Emilia, Victoria, Nadia, Misha in Durango, CO.

2024: Next generation - Hana's great-granddaughter, Emilia, with grand-daughter, Hana.

Hana Fristensky Bruce

Michael "Misha" Fristensky

Nadia Jaquez Fristensky

Chapter 14

In the Movie

Pavel Taussig was a brilliant film journalist and movie historian, and notably the author of the story for the Oscar-winning film *Kolya* (1997), which is set in Czechoslovakia. Additionally, he was the nephew of Hilda Taussigova, who was in Terezin Ghetto for three years. While there, Hilda secretly married Hanus (Jan) Sladky, who helped my mother in Terezin and also after the war. Pavel Taussig knew my mother personally. He and I had been friends for many years. We were born just a few months apart, and as babies, lived together in the same household for several months; we referred to each other as "cousins."

One spring evening in 2017 in Durango, CO, while I was researching my mother's past, my phone rang. It was Pavel Taussig, and he got right to the point. The phone call from Prague was expensive for him, so I suspected it was something important. He told me, "I just sent you an email with an attachment. It's about a fifteen-minute-long video clip. Watch it until the end." He didn't say much more. We exchanged just a few words; I didn't want to prolong the conversation much longer because of my eagerness to see what he had sent.

I sat down at my desk with intense curiosity, turned on my computer, and there in my email I had the link to the video he mentioned. It didn't take me long to get my bearings and understand what I was viewing. It was a propaganda film that the Nazis had made in the summer of 1944 in Terezin. I had already read about it in my research, but I hadn't seen it yet. I mean, I've seen only a few clips of the documentary. But not the entire movie. The complete movie has never surfaced.

I clicked the link and was glued to the monitor. Toward the end of the clip, there are sequences of the extensive gardens in the ramparts between Terezin's ghetto walls. Then there's a man wearing only short trousers who is scooping water into a watering can and is pouring water on the vegetables. And then . . . I couldn't believe my eyes . . . a close-up of a girl with short black hair, wearing a white blouse and a skirt with a pattern, watering a flower bed. My mother Hana! To make sure I wasn't imagining it, I watched it again and again, stopped it for a while, lingering, and I examined her face. I was certain that it was my mother.

Understandably, I was quite anxious. I called my wife Victoria. Of course, she knew my mom well too, and she was familiar with pictures of her from when she was younger. I didn't say anything, I just played her the film clip Taussig sent me. When it was coming to an end, Victoria's reaction was exactly the same as mine. "But that's your mom!" she exclaimed.

I stopped the movie, and we just studied my mother for a while. A beautiful young girl. She even smiled for a moment. At first glance, it showed a happy young woman tending her garden. She even says something in the film, opens her mouth, but the film didn't have authentic sound, just an accompanying commentary in the film, which at that moment was generally talking about agriculture in the ghetto. My mother! Forever immortalized in a film clip. It was one of the greatest discoveries in the search for the truth of my mother's history. Later, while visiting Terezin with my expert Terezin Ghetto guide, Lukas Lev, we even managed to find the exact spot where the Nazi propaganda film camera captured Hana's image at the age of sixteen.

The Eighth Historical Stop

Terezin Ghetto—the Potemkin Village

The Terezin film of the summer of 1944 was part of the Nazi painting of a cruel reality veneered in false imagery. It began with the first failures of the German armies on the Eastern Front, but the successful Allied campaign in North Africa also played a part. All of this also impeded the "Final Solution to the Jewish Question," which meant temporarily interrupting the transports of Terezin prisoners to camps in the East. The relevant order was issued by SS leader Heinrich Himmler himself, with the proviso to maintain the image that Terezin was a place where "Jews could live and die in peace."

The pause in the transports lasted for a full seven months and raised hopes among the prisoners that there might be a complete end to them. But it was only a temporary measure. And the pause was for a different objective than the prisoners would have wanted. The pause signaled the use of Terezin Ghetto for propaganda purposes. In the autumn of 1942, for example, pseudo-shops were opened in the ghetto where it was possible to buy goods previously confiscated/ stolen from prisoners on their arrival in the ghetto, using special vouchers. Later, a cafeteria was even opened in which prisoners, who were able to obtain tickets, were permitted an hour and a half to listen to enjoyable music and drink one substitute coffee for an hour and a half.

From the spring of 1943, the "beautification" of the town began, in order to make the ghetto sufficiently neat and orderly for foreign inspection visits. In May 1943, the Bank of the Jewish Self-government began to function, issuing practically worthless money. A little later, the streets were given names instead of the former numerical designations. Hence, for example, the former L1 Street was called Jezerni Street. At the end of June 1943, a delegation, including representatives of the German Red Cross, visited Terezin Ghetto. They were accompanied by SS officer Adolf Eichmann, who decided that it would be possible to show Terezin to a foreign visitor only after thorough preparation. In 1942, Eichmann took part in the planning for the implementation of genocide against the Jews. He was later tried and hanged in 1962.

In September, the transports resumed. In one month, 45,000 prisoners left for the East. However, there were many requests by international organizations, including the International Committee of the Red Cross, to be allowed to visit the end-sites of the deportation transports. Therefore, to appease these requests, the Nazis decided to use Terezin for propaganda purposes, which culminated during the first half of 1944. "Great attention was paid to improving the external appearance of the houses in the ghetto and the green areas. Flower beds were established in the square, and a music pavilion was built in which promenade concerts were played. A children's pavilion with indoor facilities and a playground was even built nearby. The former Sokol Hall became the Social House with halls for cultural programs, a prayer room, a library, and a restaurant terrace" (Holocaust.cz).

This effort toward the transformation of Terezin, however, also required a reduction in the number of prisoners. To accomplish this, 5,000 people were sent to Auschwitz in December 1943, and another 7,500 in May 1944. A total of 17,500 people were deported to the family camp for Terezin prisoners in Auschwitz. Of these, only 1,168 survived the liberation.

The long-prepared foreign visit to Terezin took place on June 23, 1944. It was attended by the Swiss physician Maurice Rossel, the deputy head of the International Committee of the Red Cross mission in Berlin; Frants Hvass, the representative of the Danish Foreign Ministry; and Eigil Juel Henningsen, the Danish Health Care Inspector. The delegation was accompanied by senior SS officers, as well as representatives of the German Foreign Office and the German Red Cross. This group was first received at the SS commandant's office, and from there they went to the headquarters of the Jewish Self-government, where they spoke with its leaders. The group then went on a tour of the city, during which its members addressed some of the prisoners. The scripted responses of the prisoners had been rehearsed. The visitors' walk through the ghetto was well-choreographed in advance and could not deviate from that script. The evaluation of the visit was, therefore, very satisfactory from the point of view of the SS, and the resulting report conformed to Nazi expectations. The reality, however, was that thousands of people were dying in there, and tens of thousands more were in the extermination camps in the East.

The film mentioned earlier, shot in Terezin in August and September 1944, was intended to fulfill the need for Nazi propaganda. The backdrop of the newly beautified city was used to present a fictional image of a happy life in a "Jewish settlement." Some of the prisoners, led by Kurt Gerron, were forced to participate in the filming, as they were allegedly promised that they would save their lives and the lives of their families. Gerron was a famous German actor and director of Jewish origin. Before the war, Berlin was "at his feet." He sang the original version of the well-known musical drama The Threepenny Opera *hit "Meckie Messer (Mack the Knife)," and he starred alongside Marlene Dietrich in the film* Blue Angel. *His artistic success even earned him an invitation to Hollywood.*

But Gerron stayed in Europe. The war found him in the Netherlands, where he was first interned in the Westerbork concentration camp and then transported to Terezin. In the ghetto, he founded and ran the cabaret Karusell, and in the summer of 1944, he directed the propaganda film to show a happy and fulfilling life in the Terezin Ghetto. However, the film was never officially released, and in the end, only part of it survived. Gerron was transported to Auschwitz immediately after completing his film assignment, where he and his family were murdered instantly upon their arrival. Shortly after the film was completed, many of the prisoner-actors, including the children, were also transported to Auschwitz.

I had to watch the surviving part of the film several times. It was ironically titled *Hitler Gives the Jews a City* or *Truth and Lies* (the official title was *Theresienstadt: A Documentary Film from the Jewish Settlement Areas*). Besides my mother, there are many other people in it. The footage also showed men working in the smithy and other work-shops, women at the sewing machines, a mother and child on a bench, men showering, a football match with loads of spectators, a group of women in seemingly convivial and happy conversation, and a classical music concert in a packed hall. The filmmakers, including Gerron, allegedly stretched out the filming time by demanding the same actors over and over again with the purpose of preventing and delaying transports to Auschwitz. But it was no use, because most of the performers were eventually deported to the extermination camp anyway. Fortunately, my mother was not among those deported.

In 2017, I spoke to a former Terezin prisoner, Doris Grozdanovic. We were on the site of the Terezin camp. She did not know my mother; however, later, while she was watching the movie clip with me on-site, she remembered the pretty dark-haired girl working in the garden. "I saw that Nazi propaganda film many times. I had to take care of a flock of sheep in the ghetto, and I also worked in the gardens. The young girl always fascinated me when I watched the film. I never knew who she was. I'm glad I know her identity now and that she was your mother," she told me.

Doris asked the movie operator to run the scene one more time while we were there, and she continued telling me, "She smiles very sincerely in the film; she looks happy. She was very young. Perhaps she hadn't even imagined what the future held for her and the rest of us. But I'm sure she wouldn't have smiled like that if she had been forced to. It's even possible that we met while working in the garden, but after so long, I don't remember," Doris added.

In 2011, the Swiss writer Charles Lewinsky published a great book, *Gerron*, about the making of a propaganda film and its director—part history, part fiction. "He [Gerron] was to create the biggest lie in the world. Something man must never do. He couldn't say yes, but he couldn't say no either," Lewinsky said during a visit to Prague in 2015. He tried to camouflage a message in the movie that the Nazis would not be able to decipher. "For example, he assembled a film family in the ghetto of famous people. He hoped that when someone saw the film, they would recognize the people, know that they were not really married, and understand that something was wrong." Lewinksy references in the text that follows how the German commander of Terezin at the time, Karl Rahm, briefed Gerron on the screenplay for the film:

> He was nice to me, and that's what I'm afraid of. He didn't shout at me, which would have been normal. He was polite. His tone of voice was as if he was formally addressing me. But he didn't address me that way, he wouldn't have thought of that, but he knew my name. 'You, Gerron,' he said, not 'You, Jew.' It's dangerous for a man like Rahm to know your name. 'You, Gerron,' he said, 'I have a task for you. You're going to make a film for me.' A film. At first, I thought he wanted something for himself, a film about himself—loving father Karl Rahm with his three children. Herr Obersturmführer dressed as a man. Something like that, something he could send to his family in Klosterneuburg. But Rahm has something bigger in mind. The Obersturmführer has other plans. 'Listen well, Gerron,' he begins. 'I saw a film of yours once. I don't remember what it was called, but I liked it. You're good at something. That's the nice thing about Terezin: there are a lot of people who know something. I mean, you do theater and stuff. And now I just want a film.'
>
> Then he told me what kind of film it should be. I was horrified. It must have been obvious to him, but he didn't react. Because he was counting on my dismay. Or he didn't care. I can't read faces like his. 'We've tried something along these lines before,' he said, 'but it didn't work. I was very unhappy. The people who screwed up are no longer here.'

There's always another train to Auschwitz. 'Now it's your turn,' Rahm explained, his voice still friendly. 'If you and I are lucky, something good will come of it this time. Right, Gerron?'

'I'll have to think about it,' I said to Rahm! Eppstein of the Jewish Council of Elders, who was also present at the meeting, swallowed a startled groan. A Jew has nothing to say back. Not when the camp commander wants something. The SS man who had brought me here was already reaching for a shot. I didn't see his hand; I just felt the movement. If you stand at attention, you don't turn around. Not in the camp commander's office. The wound was on its way, but Rahm waved a dismissive hand. 'He's an artist,' he said. He still looked like a friendly uncle. 'He needs inspiration. It's all right, Gerron,' he turned to me. 'I am giving you three days. To think. To make this film a success. I do not want to be unhappy with someone again. Three days, Gerron.'

I did take in punches later. Outside the door of Rahm's office. An SS man punched me in the face, like they usually do it. But not with full force. They still need me.

An accurate recap of the situation: Rahm wants me to make a film about Terezin. Not about Terezin, where I'm locked up. About Terezin they want to show the world. Like they already showed it off to the Red Cross. A happy film from a happy town. Where people go to cafes and listen to music, and play sports. Enjoying the beautiful countryside around them. Where they march cheerfully to work in the morning—hola hey, hola hey, we're cheerful, join us—and in the evening enjoy a well-deserved rest after work. A town where the streets are not lined with carts of old people who have died of hunger. That's the kind of film I'm supposed to write a screenplay for. And this is the film I'm supposed to direct. Hola hey, hola hey . . .

Rahm didn't offer me any quid pro quo. But you can't make a movie on a train to Auschwitz.

As long as I work on the film, I'll be safe. That's one side of it. The other is: walk around the swamp, you can't escape the cold. My parents were sent to Sobibor death camp. And now, I'm supposed to help them lie to the world that they're actually very nice to us? 'The smiling face of Terezin.' Rahm's own words. The smiling face of hunger, sickness and death. Directed by Kurt Gerron.

What kind of man would I be if I did that? I'd be a man who wouldn't be sent to Auschwitz. No, I'd be a man who deserves to be sent to Auschwitz. A man should know how to pray. There should be a God that we would be able to ask. But there is no God. Not even a nice one.

Following the completion of the documentary, Kurt Gerron and his wife Olga were sent from Terezin to Auschwitz, where they were killed.

Chapter 15

The Greatest Secret

Ilona Steinova-Weinstock (sister of Ela Steinova-Weissberger, who lived in Room 24) was born in the same year as my mother Hana—1928. But the two women had much more in common. In Terezin, they lived in the same barrack, L410, in the same Room 29, and even shared the same bunk bed. "I think we were very good friends. It was because we were already lying next to each other, and we talked a lot in the evenings . . . quietly. Sometimes it was very difficult to make friends because you knew that your new friend might be put on a transport to the East in the next few days—and of course, it often happened," Ilona told me during one of our conversations in 2016. By then, she had been living in the United States for a long time, following time in Israel and Brazil.

I got her phone number from her sister Ela, who also survived Terezin. Ela told me that I needed to call her sister as soon as possible. She said Ilona had a secret about my mother to share with me. When I asked her what it might be, she answered, "I do not know, because she won't tell." That sparked my curiosity, but it also made me very anxious. In the meantime, I called some other ladies (my mother's former prison-mates) on the list first, being reluctant to call Ilona. I was just procrastinating.

Finally, with much nervousness, I called Ilona. "Well, it's about time that you are calling me too! You needed to call me a long time ago," Ilona laughed into the receiver when she answered the phone. Apparently, she had already gotten the word that I would call her back. "I'm the most important one," she explained. And it was true. Ilona was probably Hana's closest friend in Terezin. They told each other everything, sharing their worries and joys. Each was "a confessional willow" for the other, a known Czech saying to describe when two friends talk about something private. I do not know if there is something similar in English. Nonetheless, very guarded secrets were indeed shared between my mother and Ilona.

The names of inhabitants from Room 29 were always changing. The girls who had been transported into the unknown were continually replaced by others. At times, the room was half-empty, and its occupants moved from bunk to bunk. "Although we shared the room with many girls, we didn't spend much time with some of them because we worked in different groups," Ilona recalled. "The exception was in the evenings, when we usually studied. There was always the fear that we might be ambushed by a German patrol. Studying was officially forbidden, but the Germans mostly turned a blind eye. Their opinion was that we were all going to die anyway, so let them have some fun for a while." Ilona, like Hana, worked in the gardens or in the fields. "It was hard, and the conditions were sometimes terrible. Hanka worked in a different group than me."

Our first phone conversation didn't go according to plan. I wasn't able to ask her about the important event or secret. Principally, she wouldn't let me ask any questions. She knew from Ela that I would ask her about the "secret," thus avoiding my direct question on this subject. Maybe she wasn't ready. She talked about meeting my mother in Prague shortly after the liberation, and mentioned their meeting in Orangeburg, NY, in 1990, including some other ladies that I didn't know. (Later, I found out that they all were former Terezin roommates.) Ilona kept talking but artfully dodged my questions. She mentioned her voyage from Prague to Israel, to Brazil, and finally to the United States. Then abruptly she said, "Time for dinner," and she hung up!

I didn't sleep too much that night. All kinds of different scenarios were floating in my head. I knew I must call again. I am sure Ilona knew that too. I gave her a few days. When I called again, I came out directly with the important question, "What is the secret?"

At that moment, Ilona paused for a minute in her recollections, like she wasn't sure if she was going to tell me. Her silence somehow scared me. She just breathed loudly as if to gather her courage. Then she spoke again. But then it was more slowly, quietly, as if she were weighing each word she spoke in her mind. "Well, you know . . ." she began, "I can't tell you . . ." And again, a brief silence, it almost felt as if she was silently weeping. And then, she continued, "I promised Hana, I wouldn't tell anyone what I know about her while I'm alive. I am that kind of person, if I promise something. I will keep that promise no matter what."

Silence. I sensed that quiet weeping again.

"I kept that promise for 72 years. But now, I know my time is running out. I'm 90, who knows how much longer I'll be around?"

Silence again. "I didn't even think I'd hear from Hanka ever again or from anyone from her family for that matter." And, she continued, "I know that she died in 1998. So maybe it's a good time to share this with you now . . . But you have to promise me something, Frank. Will you promise not to tell anyone else while I'm still alive?" I quickly promised her, having no idea where she was heading with this.

And then . . .

"You know, Hanka got married in Terezin. I think it was in '44. Her husband was a violinist, even an accomplished violinist. He came from Hungary or Slovakia. I really don't know. And I don't even remember his name. It was so long ago. And the time they could have been together was so short." Ilona paused again for a moment.

The shock of what I was hearing rendered me unable to speak.

She continued, "In Terezin, he lived in the Magdeburg barracks. He often met Hanka. That is, as much as the circumstances of Terezin allowed them. I met them both several times. Hanka was a beautiful girl, perhaps even the prettiest in our room, and he was a very handsome, charming young man. Hanka often told me about him. She was genuinely in love with him. I know she didn't even tell her family, but I was part of her secret. They were married by a rabbi according to Jewish ritual. Unfortunately, even the wedding didn't save him from being transported to Auschwitz. He left in the last wave in the autumn of 1944 transports from Terezin to Auschwitz. He didn't survive."

I don't remember exactly what I eventually said to Ilona in response to this news, but I was ready to quickly thank her for that surprising secret and urgently wanted to say goodbye to digest what I had just heard. I wanted to be by myself.

But Ilona wasn't finished yet. "Wait, that's not all," she said and paused again for a moment. "There's another part of Hanka's secret . . . and as long as I'm alive . . . Well, listen . . . Hanka got married and then found out she was pregnant . . . she was pregnant with that young violinist's child . . . only . . . well . . . she had an abortion . . ."

There was a long pause on her part, which I needed too. And then, she was closing, "So listen, you cannot talk about this, and you have to sign a paper that you are not going to publish it. In any case, I just told you a mutual agreement your mother and I had that I just shared with you. Four weeks ago, I underwent a heart surgery, and I am still recovering. I do not know if I am going to sleep tonight because of that. So, the two of us are keeping a common secret. I am hoping that you are not going to be upset that I told you this. I was debating it for the longest time if I am going to tell you or not."

My mind was numb. I really do not remember if I said anything else to her. The only thing I recall is that I was sitting downstairs in my chair for a long time. Much later, I thought about the moment when Ilona told me about the Terezin wedding, and, at first, some doubt crossed my mind. Perhaps it might not even be true? And then the pregnancy . . . I certainly couldn't blame my mother, I told myself. How could she do that? Gradually, it dawned on me. What did she have to go through every day in the ghetto? Ubiquitous poverty, disease, death, hopelessness. A life without a future. Sincere love must have been something of a heavenly miracle in such an environment.

As time went on, so much curiosity about their relationship began to stir in my mind. Were they planning a future together? Where did they want to live after the war? When and how were they going to tell their families about their relationship? Did my mother choose to have an abortion on her own, voluntarily, or was she forced into it by the German ghetto commanders? How old was she when she got married and was expecting a child? Sixteen? This was more proof that girls were becoming women much earlier in the ghetto. Was her marriage official or just for show? How did Hana cope with the distress of her abortion? It must have been a tremendous trauma at her young age.

More and more questions flooded my thoughts and emotions. And they grew prolifically when I contacted the Terezin Memorial to inquire about Hana's wedding, but there was no record of it in the surviving documents. I visited Ilona in April of 2016 in her Reseda, CA, Jewish Senior Home. It was a very emotional encounter. She was in a wheelchair, and I recognized that she didn't want to talk about what was already revealed. We had a sandwich together and talked about our kids. Ilona died in September 2019. I didn't share our secret during her lifetime.

I was unable to find out anything about my mother's first husband from Terezin, not even his name. But I continued my search. How many weddings took place in the ghetto? How many women besides Hana had become pregnant there? What about forced abortions?

I contacted Tomas Fedorovic from the Terezin Memorial Office in Terezin, who gave me basic information and other historical background. "The department of the rabbinate was responsible for the weddings in the ghetto and supplied permissions. Whether all the weddings— the official part—took place in the Magdeburg barracks is unknown to me. But congratulations and treats usually follow the wedding ceremony." Was there any other reason for the wedding besides love? Maybe protection from being sent to Auschwitz? Mr. Fedorovic continued, "Mostly it was for the sake of being assigned to a transport together, or on the contrary, as a protection against being assigned to a transport at all. If a girl married a member of AK 1 or AK 2 [the first and second transports to Terezin at the end of November and beginning of December 1941], they were protecting their wife from deportation. This protection fell in September 1943."

Still, I was determined to find out more information about this mysterious accomplished Hungarian or Slovakian musician. I gathered all the names of the 18,402 prisoners who were deported during September and October 1944 on eleven transports from Terezin to Auschwitz. Only 1,418 survived. Without knowing his name, it was a seemingly impossible task to accomplish. Maybe it's better that way.

According to available data, about 500 weddings took place in the ghetto. Several additional documents have been published that are devoted to the children born in the ghetto of Terezin, and then to the forced abortions that took place. As Mr. Fedorovic advised me, this subject was discussed in detail by historians Miroslav Karny and Margita Karna in their periodical *Terezin's Child Prisoners*, which was published years ago in the historical collection *Terezin Letters*. "The combination of the two words 'child prisoners' sounds horrible. Perhaps only the words 'prisoner from birth' can sound more horrific . . . In the Terezin concentration camp, which the Nazi organizers of the Final Solution called a 'ghetto,' there were 205, perhaps two dozen more prisoners from birth. The birth of the first of them was announced on 13 February 1942 by the daily order of the Council of Elders No. 51. It was born to the couple of Erica and Ludwig Winkler, and his name was Tomas."

Table 1. *The Age Composition of the Terezin Prisoners*

	January 1, 1943	December 31, 1943	May 31, 1944
Under 15 years	3,494	3,031	2,722
15 - 60 years	25,036	19,730	18,054
61- 65 years	4,548	3,159	2,240
Over 65 years	16,218	8,735	4,951

Source: *The Final Solution* by Miroslav Karny

The SS Camp Command initially allowed children who were conceived before the mother was imprisoned to be born. Later, births were strictly forbidden, and the births of children conceived in Terezin were judged particularly harshly. "The ban was never lifted, but later exceptions were allowed, and in the last years of the ghetto, the camp commandant no longer insisted on its observance. The image of a fictitious 'Jewish settlement' was no longer suited to the harsh enforcement of the ban on births," wrote Karny and Karna. From the report of the delegate of the International Committee of the Red Cross, Dr. Maurice Rossel, who visited Terezin on June 23, 1944, it is evident how his SS guides also lied to him on this matter. According to the SS Command, 400 children had been born in the ghetto by that time, about twice the actual number. Tomas Fedorovic from the Terezin Memorial wrote to me that there was a noticeable change in the number of births and pregnancies with the arrival of the ghetto commander Anton Burger in the summer of 1943: "He forbade persons who conceived their children in the ghetto to give birth. If they were children conceived before the deportation to the ghetto, they were allowed to remain pregnant. If a pregnancy was conceived there, not only were both parents deported, but also the attending physician. After the arrival of Commander Karl Rahm in February 1944, the situation changed, and it was possible to apply for exceptions." According to what information was available, there were approximately 350 artificially terminated pregnancies during the entire period of the ghetto's existence. One of the mothers, Ruth Wieder, gave the following testimony after the liberation:

> When I had been in a different state [pregnant] for about six months, the then ghetto commander, Anton Burger, learned about it. He constantly ordered and forced me and other women who were also in a different condition that we had to be helped away from the child. If the child was born, none of us would live—me, the child and my husband. Burger further forced me to sign some sort of declaration and agreement that if the baby was born, it would be killed immediately. I was summoned to the council of elders where I was forced to sign the statement. Burger also threatened us that if we did not sign this declaration, I would be immediately put on a transport to Auschwitz. Before I signed the declaration, I and about ten other women who were in a different condition went to ask Burger to give us permission to give birth as an exception. He replied that he didn't want to hear about it. Later, however, he did allow the births. My child was stillborn, but the nine other women had live children. These women and their children were, as I know, sent straight to Auschwitz to be gassed.

So, Ruth Wieder was saved because she had a stillborn child. On November 24, 1943, Terezin prisoner Egon Redlich wrote, "They made us sign that we agreed to kill our child. Fear, fear reigns. Fear and terror turn people into evil animals. What am I saying? Even animals don't kill their children. What do they make of us? . . . I signed the killing of my child ... They kill the children in their stomachs, but they command us to improve the city."

Pregnancy was strictly controlled in the Terezin camp. Reports of the birth of a child had to be submitted regularly, and every case of a discovered pregnancy, especially those in Terezin, had to be reported. Neglect of the reporting obligation was severely punished, usually by death. In fact, a circular dated August 21, 1943, addressed to the chief physicians and gynecologists made it clear: "On the occasion of the reporting of the last two births, Herr SS-Obersturmfuhrer Burger announced that henceforth all fathers of children conceived here, as well as the mother and child, would be included in the transport and would be removed. We, therefore, ask once again that all pregnancies known to you, if they have not yet been reported, be reported, since the failure to report becomes an accomplice of the examining female doctor. The communication to pregnant women must be completely unequivocal, and the termination of pregnancy must be carried out by official order." The directive of March 18, 1944, barracks' leaders says, "All female residents must be reminded. All women of the years 1928 to 1889 must certify in writing on their papers that they have been instructed to report to the appropriate women's dispensary immediately at the first sign of pregnancy for examination. If there are cases of pregnancy being concealed, the custodian of the rooms must expect to be held accountable in the future in view of the reporting obligation."

I am not sure if my mother reported her pregnancy or how she proceeded with an interruption to her pregnancy. But according to the available literature concerning this matter, she and the abortion-executing doctor must have reported this procedure to the ghetto's authorities.

In direct contrast to the secret I had discovered about my mother—that she had married and even become pregnant in the ghetto—I had a second revelation. Or was it, on the contrary, in harmony with it? Hana had let it be known shortly after the war that she did not want any children; she revealed this sentiment to Pavel Taussig. She was traumatized by her experience in the ghetto. Due to the need to sanitize all the rooms, Hana and all the girls had moved from L410, where girls her age lived, to a house with grown women. There, she witnessed these respectable married women having sex with their lovers. Sex was ubiquitous. And more or less public. In a world where tomorrow was not guaranteed, living for the moment was all some of them had.

"Hanka was really traumatized by it," Pavel Taussig told me years later. "She said the women were really having the time of their lives." It must have been a harsh reality for a young, sensitive girl in love with a handsome violinist. It was difficult enough for her to deal with her pregnancy, her abortion. Here the most intimate communication between two people was overt and commonplace, part of the everyday life in Terezin. Hana saw it every day. It was unavoidable. The images of people having sex must have been deeply etched in her memory. She didn't want to be like them. But fate willed it otherwise.

After the war, Hana met the young Jaromir Fristensky in Moravia. And it didn't take long for my mother to get pregnant, for the second time, in fact, and it was me who was about to be born . . .

But let's not get ahead of ourselves.

Chapter 16

To Auschwitz

Living in Terezin was like playing the most dramatic game of roulette. The stakes were not for money, but for human life. In the autumn of 1944, practically anyone could have been assigned to one of the transports to Auschwitz. More than 18,000 Terezin prisoners left the ghetto in a single month, and only a fraction of them lived to see liberation. Hana experienced incredible fear. Will I get a travel voucher now? Or my mother, father, brother? My husband?

The beginning of the year promised nothing pleasant. It was so cold. It was almost impossible to sleep. The small stove in the room didn't produce enough heat. Not only that, but there also wasn't enough burning material such as wood or coal. It had to be stolen from somewhere, which was dangerous. Moreover, in February, there was no heating at all, because everything that could be burned just wasn't available anywhere in the entire ghetto. In addition, much of the major food supply ran out. Some old potato skins were mixed in the something-like-a-soup, which made some of the food somewhat bearable. Occasionally, there was goulash, dumplings with sugar, or buns.

In March, Hana and the other girls, who worked in agriculture, did get a little more bread, sometimes even bread rolls and jam. Despite the inclement weather, Hana and her fellow inmates had to work from seven in the morning until five in the evening, sometimes even longer. They planted lettuce, kohlrabi, cabbage, composted, and transported soil from one place to another. It was very hard work. All day long they were in the cold mud or snow, soaked and frozen to the bone. None of the girls was adequately dressed for these kinds of conditions. The coal supply for the stove finally arrived, but the coldest part of winter was nearly over. Sleeping was almost impossible anyway, due to the constant attacks of bedbugs and other vermin.

Hana was strengthened by encounters with her love (the violinist), whom she would marry that year, and also by meetings with her brother, Petr. She met with each of them as often as possible, as well as with her mother and father. At the beginning of June, the news spread through Terezin that the Allies had landed in France. It was as if someone had thrown the water of life on the prisoners. The optimism was palpable. There was such hope that the war would soon be over! The hopefulness was further boosted by the sound and sight of Allied bombers repeatedly flying overhead on their way to Germany. Many inmates of the ghetto even began to exhibit hints of a smile again after long months. The Nazis were trying to suppress any such good news for the prisoners. But they couldn't stop it, because the business of smuggling information was flourishing. However, the hellish ordeal was far from over.

Then came the end of September . . . and with it, the beginning of what would be the final round of deportations to Auschwitz. On September 28, 1944, on transport train number Ek 802, Petr was among 2,499 prisoners on board. (I later found out my friend Arnost Lustig was also included. Only 382 survived.) Hana only realized this two days later, when Petr did not show up for their regular meeting. She panicked. She did not want to go to her parents, so she went to her friend Hilda Taussigova-Sladka, who confirmed Petr's departure. Hilda tried to console Hana for a long time before they parted, but it didn't help much. Hana was overcome by a hellish fear that she couldn't shake. She had a sickening feeling. Who's next? The transports were leaving for Auschwitz now almost every other day, as the Nazis were feeling the squeeze on both the Eastern and Western fronts. They knew that the end could be near. But when? Thousands of people were suddenly gone forever.

Hana's friends and acquaintances shared the same emotions. The earlier hopes for a happy ending were gone with the deportations. While their early knowledge of what the transports meant was filled with uncertainty, it became clear later that the deportations most certainly were met with deadly outcomes. There was nervousness in the ghetto. Fear. Anxiety. No one was certain if they would stay. Earlier, some prisoners had enjoyed the privilege of not being included in the transport; now any protection was removed. They were all exposed. Then came more devastation from which Hana would not soon recover. The first great love of her life, her Terezin husband, was selected for transport to Auschwitz. He got into a cattle truck among 1,500 prisoners, and suddenly he was gone. In the evening, when Hana found out, she crawled into a corner of the room, curled up in a ball, and cried for a long time. The tears would not stop.

In days of total uncertainty, her mother, Marta, went to see her friend, Hilda Taussigova-Sladka, with whom she worked in the same kitchen. Since they had become very good friends, she asked Hilda if she would take care of Hana if she and her husband were also put on a transport. She also asked her not to tell her daughter the day of their eventual departure.

Hilda grabbed Marta's hands and reassuringly told her, "Don't worry, Marta, I'll take care of her. But I'm sure it won't be necessary; you will stay here with your family." She tried to give my grandmother some sense of comfort.

Hilda met Hanus Sladky in 1942, and they soon fell in love. Hanus was one of the first Terezin prisoners on duty, having arrived in Terezin on November 24, 1941, in the very first "work-commando," named AK 1 transport. This work-commando was preparing the former military and wooden barracks for the influx of prisoners. Hanus and Hilda met while she was working in the kitchen. "In December 1942, Hilda and her parents, Gustav and Pavla Taussig, were assigned to a transport to the East. I offered Hilda that I would marry her so that she could stay in Terezin as a family member of a privileged member of AK 1. Thus, at the beginning of December, the wedding took place and Hilda stayed with me in Terezin," wrote Hanus Sladky in his memoirs after the war. It was through his wife, Hilda, that Hanus met Hana and her parents. According to his memories, Hana was also supposed to be deported to Auschwitz in October 1944. "She received a transport order for one of the first transports in October 1944. Mr. and Mrs. Klein were not affected," Hanus wrote. "Mr. Klein stirred up all his contacts to remedy this unusual division of the family. His efforts were successful, and Hanka was able to stay with her parents." But it didn't end there.

According to Hanus, Rudolf and Marta Klein were included in the next transport on October 16, 1944, with transport numbers Er 584 and Er 585 among 1,500 prisoners to Auschwitz (only 117 survived). This time, Rudolf's effort to keep the whole family together was not successful. "The day after the transports departed, I met Hanka on the street. I asked her what had happened and learned that her parents had been sent to Auschwitz, and she had to stay in the ghetto. She was left alone, and I invited her to come to us [Hanus and Hilda lived together as a couple] whenever she wants. She came to us more and more often, daily toward the end of the war," Hanus wrote in his memoirs. Hilda fulfilled her promise, and she really took care of Hana, not only in the ghetto, but after the war as well.

According to another version, which was told to me decades after the war by one of Hana's former prison-friends, the departure for Auschwitz took a slightly different course. Supposedly, Hana and her father, Rudolf, were included in the transport, but not Hana's mother, who still worked in the kitchen. When Marta found out that Hana was on the deportation list, she went to the ghetto office and put herself on the list instead of her daughter. When Hana found out, her parents were already in the cattle truck; she ran after the departing train, watching it disappear in the distance.

Incredible coincidences, luck, sacrifice, and instinct often decided who would or would not be included in the transport. Hanus Sladky himself experienced something like this in the autumn of 1944. At that time, the SS command was having a building on the square rebuilt, and Hanus was given the task of re-installing central heating in a few rooms. The working days were fourteen hours. The prisoners were supervised by the SS-Unterscharfuhrer Rudolf Haindl. But those fourteen hours were too much for Hanus. Since he excelled at his job, he finished each day after eight hours. After a few days, however, Haindl became suspicious. He asked Hanus where he was going so soon.

"Instinctively, I replied that in welding, the working time affects the quality of the seams. Eight hours is the maximum if I want to prevent leaks. Haindl let me go without reacting, but in the following days, he stood next to me and checked whether I was really working continuously for eight hours," recalled Hanus. Almost all of his acquaintances had already received their orders to be deported to Auschwitz by that time or had already left. Some of those who were designated as reserves were not allowed to leave their dwellings so they could be included in the transport as needed if someone on the original list was dropped for any reason. Hanus was also informed that he was placed in reserve for the next transport.

"The next morning, I did not know what to do, whether to stay in my room and be ready when called, or to go to work and disobey the order to stay in the quarters. I decided to go to the construction site, where Haindl shouted at me for being late. Instead of explaining, I handed him the draft order. He read it and said, 'Keep working.' So, I continued my work, and Haindl disappeared. The next day, an acquaintance told me that Haindl had taken me out of all transports," noted Hanus. Because of this Haindl situation, Hanus and his wife Hilda survived the October transports, which were the last ones out of the ghetto. Hanus's mother, however, was not so lucky. "She was included in the last transport from Terezin to Auschwitz on October 28, 1944, and I never saw her again."

Hana was never to see her parents again, but she did not fully comprehend the permanence of that in the autumn of 1944. She clung to the hope that she would be reunited later with her parents, her brother, and her husband. Life doesn't have to be all tragic, she consoled herself. But that attempt at comforting herself was temporary. It was devastating for her to face the reality that within a few days, she had lost all her loved ones who had left the ghetto. At one point, it even occurred to her that life didn't really matter. She began to reproach herself for not leaving too. Why was I spared and they were not? Why did I deserve such a different fate? I'm not any better than my mother, or my father, or my brother . . . Why? Suddenly, nothing was important. Nothing made sense.

Hana's friends from Room 29, the ones who remained, helped her to cope. There weren't many left anymore. The room was unusually empty after the last October transports. The visual of many spare beds was a stark contrast to the earlier days of close quarters, and there were reminders of the many memories of the girls, behind whom the heavy transport carriage doors had closed. It was all so swift. There was no time to say goodbye. Get on! Departure! The whole ghetto, ironically, was half empty. Where there used to be heads on heads, suddenly it was unusually desolate. The remaining girls in Room 29 showed themselves to be real comrades. Most of them had lost their parents and other relatives; most of them had to face being left alone. It brought them all even closer together. They bonded together. They encouraged each other. They cried together when they couldn't stand it anymore. After a few days, one of the guardians, who had been in charge of the young girls, appeared in Room 29. He told them they could move in with their parents or some of their relatives if they were still alive. Hana had nowhere to go. Neither did most of the other girls. They stayed for each other.

Alena Taussig, the mother of the aforementioned Pavel Taussig, told me years ago that Hana had told her practically nothing about her horrible experience in Terezin. "And I didn't ask her about it. Yet I felt that she was still struggling with the suffering. Only once, when we talked about Hana's brother Petr, did she confide in me, 'Life in Terezin was horrible.' But the worst part was the uncertainty of the next day. Waiting to see what would happen the next day. No one could know."

That was the Nazi's psychological demolition.

Chapter 17

Escape from Terezin

One early morning in April 1945, Hana suddenly woke up and sprang up on the bunk bed, alarmed and looking around. It was still dark outside. Suspicious noises were filtering into the room, the familiar sound of gunshots. They were heavy weapons barrages from a distance. Cannons? Hana listened intently. She woke Ilona, who was sleeping next to her. "Ilona, Ilona, listen, do you hear that?!" Ilona raised herself sleepily on her elbows but shook her head, expressing that she heard nothing. But then it came again. Was it really artillery fire? They had never heard anything quite like that before. Who was firing? How far away from here? More girls woke up, and some jumped out of bed and ran to the window.

"Don't look out, they'll start shooting at you!" Hana heard one of her roommates say. After a while, the sounds of artillery fire died down, but none of the girls fell asleep again. Hana felt her heart pounding. Did this mean the end of the nightmare was finally near?

Hana was no longer living in the girls' building L410 at that time; it had been cleared out in February 1945, and the girls had moved to a building marked L414. But their morning was the same as the other days. The girls performed their obligatory cleaning routine, but the tension in the room was felt everywhere. They went down-stairs, lined up in the courtyard of L414 to go to work. The darkness was slowly changing to daylight. During the walk, none of the girls dared to mention the experience of the early morning hours. None of them knew the Red Army had already liberated a significant part of pre-war Czechoslovakia. None of them could suspect the fall of the Terezin Ghetto was very imminent.

It was evident to the girls in the days that followed that something was happening. The harsh orders and strict daily regime that had been embedded in daily life for the last few years were disappearing and were being replaced by organized chaos. All the inhabitants of the ghetto, young and old, were doing their best just to survive. Now more than ever, their desire to live was extraordinary; they had a desire to leave this atrocious place, to be free and to reunite with their loved ones. And for that they needed food, water, and other things. Now they had to show the Nazis that they had endured, that they had survived, that it was impossible to exterminate them all.

Hana was no longer working in the gardens, but she was doing what was needed. The girls were sent where some necessary work was required. Hana was among girls she didn't know, but she didn't mind. After all these years, she was used to change. She was hardened. Her parents and her brother were gone, yet she still continued to believe that she would see them again after the war, that they would all be together again. She imagined falling into their arms. She also thought of her beloved husband, with whom she planned to live after the war, and of the other family members who had been in the ghetto and who may have either died or left in transports. But right now, she was left all alone.

How much longer will we be here? When will the war finally end? When will I be able to go home? More and more of these and other questions dominated her thoughts, but nobody knew the answers. Hana tried to imagine her future, but there was only an impenetrable fog over what lay ahead. When she was working, she managed to suppress her thoughts, she didn't have to think . . . to think about what was going to happen. The more work, the better for me, Hana told herself.

The days passed quickly, but the evenings were different. There was no escaping the painful thoughts that inevitably invaded any solitude. Hana was no longer the innocent little girl who had come to the ghetto with her doll. Suddenly she was a young woman, even though she was not yet officially an adult. "Maybe it was all just a bad dream that will dissolve when I wake up," she used to say to herself as she lay down at night and closed her eyes. She thought of her husband. What might he be doing at that moment? Where was he now? Was he alive? Would she ever see him again? She really loved him. She really did. With all her heart. When they were still together, she experienced feelings she'd never known. In the midst of total devastation, total insecurity, fear, misery—a feeling of happiness. These brief moments, despite their short duration, were so liberating. When Hana could hold those moments in her heart and mind, she faintly smiled. But then her thoughts turned back to the reality of Terezin, to the evil of Terezin. A cruel contrast.

Many of her friends had left the ghetto with the last transports, but fortunately, Ilona, whom Hana considered one of her best friends, stayed behind. A few other friends also remained. Ilona and Hana shared the top bunk bed. Lying there next to each other, they talked together more often. Their mental and physical tiredness did not matter. Ilona kept Hana's secret, which she promised never to tell anyone . . . ever: the secret of her great love that ended in pregnancy and . . . abortion. They lay together on the bed on their backs, staring at the ceiling. They spoke quietly about places they had never been, making up what they might have looked like. They heard the music they had experienced with the other prisoners at the modest yet unforgettable concerts in the basement of their former home in L410 or in the attic of the Hanover Barrack. They recalled Ilona's sister, Ela, performing as the Cat in all 55 performances of the children's opera *Brundibar*. They heard Verdi's *Requiem* or Smetana's *The Bartered Bride* playing in their heads again. Sometimes they talked about their families, whom they would surely meet again after the war. How much they believed it! They helped each other to suppress the thought that it might not be so.

Each day was a rollercoaster of emotions: experiencing any kind of solace or hope, and then just as quickly, being thrown back into the depths of heavy-heartedness. To counterbalance the depths of the darkness and to bolster the need for optimism, even small bits of positive news were eagerly consumed. One morning in April, Hana and Ilona met with Ela, who shared news of her own mother's health. It was a relief for Ilona to learn her mother seemed to be recovering well from an injury she had sustained a few weeks earlier when she had fallen down the stairs in her barracks. The impact of this information was enough sustenance for the heart to help them get through the day. They were all starved for any kind of compassion or motivation to be strong.

After the news from Ela, Hana then waited for the other girls. They received their work orders, and most of them went in different directions. Later that afternoon, she met Hilda Taussigova-Sladka and Hanus Sladky at the corner of Jager and Lange streets. Since the deportation of her parents to Auschwitz in September 1944, Hana met Hilda quite often. Hilda was fulfilling the promise she had made to Marta that she would take care of her daughter.

Another example of the slight details of the day that raised spirits was any offering of atypical foods. At the beginning of April, a special committee arrived in the ghetto delivering rice, cheese, sugar, and chocolate. "We young people got the most," one of Hana's friends happily recalled years later.

In mid-April, news spread throughout the ghetto that the war was over. The girls ran out into the street and started singing and dancing, when suddenly SS men on horses appeared and herded everyone back inside. The girls ran to their rooms in fear. Another abrupt drop in the rollercoaster that dictated emotions.

But the war really wasn't to last much longer. "We were lying on the bunk bed in the evening, and I said to Hanka, 'It's my birthday on the 5th of May. It definitely will be the end of the war,'" Ilona told me years later in her Jewish senior home in Los Angeles. Her prediction missed the liberation of the ghetto by only a few days.

The Ninth Historic Stop

Typhus Replaced the Nazis

In the autumn of 1944, the fronts from the East (Russians) and West (the Allies) were approaching the German border unstoppably. Nevertheless, the extermination machine of the Nazis was still running at full speed. Between September 28 and October 28, 1944, 18,000 people, including representatives of the Terezin's Jewish self-government and their families, were placed on transports from Terezin to Auschwitz. "The SS commandant cynically offered women the opportunity to join their previously deported husbands. They then volunteered to join the transports with their children and left for their deaths," from the Terezin Memorial website. Only 1,574 of them were liberated.

One of the reasons for the deportation of such a large number of working age Terezin prisoners was that Nazis feared a possible uprising in the Bohemian and Moravian Protectorate, as evidenced by a letter from SS and Gestapo chief

Heinrich Himmler to Protectorate State Minister Karl Hermann Frank, in which he wrote about the need for preventive measures.

About 11,000 prisoners remained in Terezin, but from December onwards thousands more began to arrive in the ghetto—for example, Slovak and Hungarian Jews, members of mixed marriages from the Protectorate, and, as the front advanced, people from the so-called evacuation transports, from concentration camps cleared during the retreat from the advancing Red Army. Some prisoners thus appeared in Terezin a second time—after the transport to Auschwitz, they were marked as fit for work during the infamous selection process by Dr. Mengele, and thus escaped the gas chamber. All of them in the arriving transports were starved and impoverished, with many on the verge of death, while others were already dead.

As the Allied front approached, Himmler began to use Jewish prisoners as capital for negotiations with the Allies. And so it was that on February 2, a group of 1,200 Terezin prisoners left for Switzerland. Many refused the offer to travel to a safe country because they did not believe the train was heading to Switzerland and refused to leave Terezin. The transport, however, truly went to Switzerland. One of my mother's friends, Eva Steinova-Klinger, was on that transport. Following her timely recovery in Switzerland, she moved to Brazil. Eva and her two daughters visited Hana in her home in Switzerland in the mid-1980s. In early April 1945, a second delegation of the International Committee of the Red Cross arrived in Terezin, preceded by a month-long "beautification" of the ghetto. It was not much help for the Nazis, however, because the propaganda use of the "model ghetto" was ruined by the rapid ending of the war.

In mid-April, another rescue convoy followed—this time, buses from the Swedish Red Cross took a group of Danish Jews to Scandinavia. At the end of April, the wives and children of SS members and part of the SS service left Terezin.

The prisoners from the evacuation transports that arrived from the East were infested with dangerous contagious diseases, especially typhus. The first case was recorded on April 24, and then the disease began to spread in tidal wave proportions. Even the original Terezin inhabitants could not escape it. On the second day of May, a delegation from the International Committee of the Red Cross arrived in Terezin and took control of the ghetto. After burning most of the compromising documents, the last SS men left a few days later. However, retreating Wehrmacht and SS units continued to move around Terezin, threatening the prisoners with gunfire—and actually killing several people. The first Red Army troops passed through Terezin on the afternoon of May 8.

In Terezin at that time, the fight against the typhus epidemic continued despite all measures to stop the spread. On May 4, a group of Czech doctors and medics from the Czech Auxiliary Action arrived in the ghetto. Five Soviet field hospitals with mobile field hospitals, as well as deworming stations and bathrooms, arrived in Terezin. Other medics and volunteers arrived. Among them was Czech silver screen star Natasha Gollova, who contracted the disease while helping the sick. The Jewish doctors and health workers continued to bear the force of the struggle against the epidemic, which peaked between May 6 and 16. Due to the strength of the epidemic, Terezin was sealed off, and a two-week quarantine was declared. From May 20, the number of infected began to decrease, and by the end of May, it was possible to give permission for some of the prisoners to return to their barracks. The epidemic had claimed more than 1,500 lives of former ghetto residents, including 34 Jewish health workers. Several medical workers from the Czech Relief Action also died, as well as Soviet personnel.

During the epidemic, the first prisoners escaped from Terezin. More left immediately after the liberation of the ghetto. Organized repatriation began at the end of May, with Czechoslovakian nationals leaving first, and, later, foreign prisoners as well. In the meantime, the camp was maintained by former prisoners. "Many of them postponed their departure from the places of former suffering for weeks and months in order to help their sick and exhausted co-prisoners," from the Terezín Museum website. Beginning June 19, 1945, the official name of the ghetto was "Former Concentration Camp, Terezin-City." Many Polish, German, and Austrian Jews refused to return to their home countries, fearing what might be there for them, and they immediately asked to be deported to America or Palestine. These people did not leave Terezin until July and August 1945.

As April drew to a close, the German guards were understandably becoming increasingly nervous and irritable, so they packed up what they could. The formerly perfect and well-oiled machine of the organization of work suddenly slowed. News leaked into the ghetto that the Russians were already outside Berlin. The bravest prisoners left the ghetto secretly. Their relatives even came to Terezin to pick them up. Freedom, freedom. Even Hana couldn't wait! She was also thinking of escaping ... "But it didn't go as fast as we wanted," Hana's friend Vera Bendova-Gulikova recalled years later. According to Vera's testimony, Hana was destined to work in the so-called "Schleuse." This was the place where she sorted the personal belongings of people who arrived in Terezin at the end of the year from other camps in the East, where the Red Army was approaching. "Since no new transports had arrived since the autumn of 1944, Hanka had more free time. Of course, we were all envious of her. That was until April 19, 1945, when Hanka was ordered to report to the 'Schleuse' again the next day. She had to leave the room as early in the morning as the rest of us. We spent a relatively quiet day in the gardens of Terezin, and by four in the afternoon, we were home again. Hanka was already there, sitting on the bed, obviously upset and frightened," Vera said. When the other girls asked her what had happened, she just shook her head in denial. "I still remember her anxious look and then her quiet, muffled voice when she finally spoke," Vera recalled.

According to Hana, Vera continued, the morning was like any other. The girls met up, and the group leader took them to the railway line where the freight cars were already lined up. Hana found it strange that no one was getting off. "The guards then unchained the locks of the cars, and then ordered us to open the doors to assist the people in getting out," Hana spoke in a quiet voice to her friends. "We tried to open the door, but it wouldn't open, it was like something was pushing on the door from the inside and . . . ." Hana broke down crying. Big tears ran down her cheeks. One of the girls took her in her arms to comfort her. Everyone around waited impatiently for her to continue. Hana calmed down a bit and continued, "Finally, we managed to open the sliding doors . . . and . . . dead bodies started falling out of the wagons . . . at our feet corpses were falling on us . . . there were corpses everywhere . . . the whole train was full of corpses." Hana and the other girls had to carry the lifeless bodies away on the carts that were usually used to carry bread.

"With the girls in the room, we looked in disbelief at each other," Vera recalled. "No one said anything. There were only sobs." Hana never forgot the falling corpses. She had that image of the absolute apocalypse, the image of the Final Solution, in its most horrifying form, etched deep in her memory. How could such a thing ever happen?

Years later, in Tel Aviv, one of the survivors, Maud Stecklmacherova-Beer, added even more horrific details to this terrible episode. "The lined-up wagons in front of the Hamburg barracks were full of mutilated corpses. There were only a few survivors, who didn't even look human. They ate the flesh of the dead; they were so starving."

At the end of April, typhus began to spread through the ghetto. Hana and several other girls were to report to one of the barracks where sick prisoners were lying. The girls were instructed to stay away from the infected and to serve them only sweetened tea. They were not allowed to give them any food, not even a piece of bread, because it would have a fatal impact on them. When they returned to their room after this service, Ilona confided to the other girls in a sad voice that a sick man motioned to her for something to eat. He was already so ill that he could not speak. But she had to follow the strict instructions, and she agonized over refusing to feed him, knowing he would likely die.

The next day, the girls were again on duty in the typhoid ward. They were afraid to go in, but they knew they had to, that it was their duty to help. They hoped that liberation was just around the corner and that soon they would not have to look at the sick, emaciated, ashen-colored bodies where every bone was visible or at victims' terrified bulging eyes. Hana was horrified at the thought of running into any of her relatives among the sick. Dark thoughts of her parents and Petr immediately overcame her, and she tried to dismiss that possibility. Amidst all the horror, every now and then there was a patient who began to recover—they were no longer just a skeleton covered with skin and completely apathetic and immobile. They were slowly becoming a person with a soul again.

The thunderous gunshots Hana and Ilona heard that night were getting closer and closer. Word spread among the prisoners that the Russians were very near, that they would arrive in a few days. But many of the inhabitants of the ghetto did not see it coming. People were dying every day; food was scarce; sanitary conditions had collapsed. But the hope in their hearts continued to survive. At the beginning of May, a commission of the International Red Cross arrived and took over the administration of the ghetto. In the following days, more and more doctors and nurses began to arrive in the ghetto, so that Hana and the other girls no longer had to return to the makeshift hospital. What a relief it was for everyone!

A few days later, Hana and her friends found out that all the SS men had left Terezin. They had left behind a grave of ashes from the burned documents. The number of people infected with typhus was growing. Hana was confused and uncertain what to do next. Should she run away? Stay put? Around Terezin were still-operating retreating units of the German Wehrmacht. On May 6, a friend from another room of their barrack told Hana she was planning to leave the ghetto in a few days. That conversation helped Hana in her final decision to leave as well. She knew that Vera and Alena, her friends from the same room, were also organizing an escape. The girls met several times and discussed when and how they would carry out their plan. At one meeting, Hana asked how they would get to Prague once they were outside the ghetto walls. Vera replied with a grin, "We are going to hitchhike."

Two days later, the first Red Army tanks arrived to help the Prague Uprising. The girls decided the next day would be the day to leave their abominable home. Their excitement kept them from sleeping. Would they manage to get out of the ghetto, which was closed because of the typhus epidemic, and everyone inside was quarantined? At dawn, they packed their bags. It didn't take long. They didn't have much with them anyway. They packed some more food and headed southeast—the opposite direction from the way they had arrived in the ghetto three years ago. Then it was a march into the unknown, an exciting escape from hell. Vera, Alena, and Hana gradually made their way through the prepared hole in the fence next to the wall. They grasped each other's hands as they helped one another out. Hana's heart was pounding; she looked around quickly and was out. She was free!

In tears, the girls all hugged each other, but there was little time to enjoy their sudden freedom. They had to get away as quickly as possible. They all ran toward the road leading to Prague. They ran so fast they soon were forced to stop to catch their breath. They sensed their destination was close. They were still breathing heavily. Were they running out of steam or had their inner excitement and nervousness taken over? After three long years, they were suddenly swept by a totally new feeling. Hana asked Vera, "What are we going to do now?" as the girls were standing under a large tree near the road from Litomerice.

It took Vera some time before she answered that important question. In that pause, the answer appeared miraculously, one that instilled the hope they needed. "Look up the street," she said, pointing. They saw military trucks, as well as tanks and other equipment, driving along the road. As the girls stood a short distance from the road, they saw an approaching convoy of trucks and could feel the wind of the passing vehicles in their hair. But suddenly they froze.

Vera stepped closer to the asphalt and started waving at the passing cars. "Watch out, don't let something run you over," she said to her friends with a wide smile. Vera hadn't been joking a few days earlier when she suggested to her friends that they would actually be hitchhiking. And they were lucky—soon, one of the mud-covered trucks with a red star on the door stopped. A Soviet soldier sitting next to the driver jumped out of the car, smiled, and asked the girls in broken German where they were going. They replied in unison, "To Prague!" And then the girls smiled too. The soldier gestured for them to get in. Soon, the truck started its journey to the capital. On the way, they passed by tanks and other army equipment.

The cab was silent. The driver took a drag from his cigarette and hardly looked at the girls. Hana could finally calm down after the tension of the past few moments. And then her mind raced as it had on so many other occasions. She had arrived in Terezin three years ago as a fourteen-year-old girl who no longer existed.

The doll was gone. Her family was gone. There was no one's hand to hold. She was now a young woman and alone. How could she even relate to those her own age who had not endured what she had in the hell of the concentration camp? Three years seems like a short episode in the span of a human life. But for a teenage girl, it is almost an eternity. For Hana it was three years of stolen youth never to be returned.

Her joyless contemplation was interrupted by Alena, who nudged Hana and pointed to the crowd of listless German soldiers marching on the side of the road in the opposite direction. They had no weapons; some of them wore torn and dirty uniforms; their heads were bowed in surrender. Hana suddenly felt an overwhelming anger and adrenaline that caused her heartbeat and breathing to quicken. The anger was welling up inside her. *What had I done to them? What was I guilty of?*

At that moment, she thought of her parents and brother again. The consistent and frequent self-assuring affirmation again was raised: surely, they would all meet again in Prague. She didn't want to admit to herself that one of the wagons with dead bodies that had arrived in April from the camps in the East might have contained the bodies of her family. She pushed aside the thought and smiled at the driver who had just offered the girls water. They all eagerly took it and quenched their thirst both literally and figuratively. Their throats were dry after the emotionally-charged escape from Terezin, and they longed to discover what the future held for each of them.

But the relief didn't end with water. The chauffeur then offered them a cigarette. The girls looked at each other questioningly, and then each took one out of the crumpled box. Why not light up when they were free? They knew very well what rare commodity cigarettes were in the ghetto. They also didn't want to offend the soldier who was taking them to Prague. None of them had smoked before. The cabin of the truck was soon full of smoke, as the girls coughed and gasped. The chauffeur laughed and motioned for them not to throw the sticks out of the window. They also understood from his words that they were approaching the vicinity of Prague, where he would let them go. He also warned them to be careful because there might still be shooting in the city. With thanks and grins, the girls jumped out of the vehicle.

Suddenly, Prague appeared before them. They could see the churches' spirals. They could see the city where they were born—their home again. Real home. Hana felt elation pulsing through her whole body. She smiled and looked at her fellow travelers. Vera and Alena were also laughing. Hana pinched her arm to make sure she wasn't dreaming. It was true! Everything would be all right now, she thought. No more bunk beds, lice, and fleas, water instead of soup, and freezing in the garden. And mostly she was grateful for no more fear of being put on the transport and losing family members and friends. There is peace at last!

The girls looked at each other, and Alena asked, "But what if some checkpoint stops us and finds we have no personal papers?"

Vera replied, "I'm sure he'll know from our appearance where we're running away from." The girls just shrugged and waved their hands.

The road sloped down a hill where they could see the Vltava River. With their eyes, the girls devoured everything that suddenly seemed so beautiful and free. Even the air smelled fresh and unspoiled. It was a beautiful spring day, May 9, 1945. The young women stood at the intersection of two streets. They heard gunshots in the distance and saw people walking by, some holding rifles. It gave them all pause. Was this just a momentary relief? There was still some fighting in Prague, but they were out of Terezin. Now it was up to each of them to fend for themselves.

Vera wanted to go to Zizkov, where her mother lived. She was a Christian who had married a Jewish man. Alena went the same way. Hana planned to go in the direction of Old Town Square. They all embraced one last time . . . long, sincere hugs. Would they ever see each other again? Tears appeared in their eyes. They wished each other good luck. "Take a deep breath, and you'll be fine," one of them assured the others, and they all responded with laughter. Then they split up and went their separate ways.

Hana headed for 17 Norimberk Street (today Paris Street), where her uncle Dr. Arthur Aschermann's family lived, at least what she believed to still be true. Hopefully, things remained reasonably unchanged. She walked down toward the Vltava River to cross over one of the bridges to the other side. When she reached the edge of the bridge, she saw a barricade on the other side. Hana was frightened, so she decided to cross the Vltava River on the next bridge. She walked at a fast pace for a while, with the Vltava River on her left side, but then she had to stop. She rested, leaning over the railing and observing the slowly flowing river. The small waves were reflecting the sun's silvery beams right at her. She felt hot, and she was breathing heavily, bathing joyfully in that feeling. Before the war, she used to go to the river and splash her feet in the waves. But that was then, when life was normal. She picked herself up from her reverie and started walking again.

Other people passed her, occasionally glancing at each other in an almost accusatory manner. Could they tell I was coming back from the ghetto? To avoid any scrutiny, Hana walked even faster, and soon she was approaching the Old Town Square. As she walked, surrounded by the historic buildings, she couldn't believe her eyes. Part of the Old Town Hall had been burnt down, and there was no glass in the windows. The houses and the square showed evidence of gunshots and grenades; there was rubble everywhere. Hana sat down on the steps of St. Nicholas Church and watched the bustle in the square. Despite the scars of war all around, she thought that people were happy, friendly. She knew she was only a short walk away from Uncle Arthur's apartment. There she hoped to see him, his wife Anna, who was an Aryan, and their daughter Maria, whom they all called Mancina. Even though Mancina was seven years older than her, they had spent much time together before the war. Mancina was a bit of a babysitter for her and Petr, often going on trips to the Czech countryside with the whole Klein family.

She wondered what it would be like to be with the Aschermanns. How would they welcome her? Sitting on the steps, she was so absorbed in her thoughts she did not notice an older woman who approached her and began to speak to her. Hana was startled and sprang up. Her jumpiness was an instinctive reaction from her life in Terezin. Sitting on the street in the ghetto would have called for a punishment. "Just stay seated, young lady," the old woman gently instructed; she had a comforting expression. This took Hana by surprise. It had been so very long since she had been treated with such compassion by a stranger. No one in Terezin addressed her that way. She was confused. She didn't know what to do, so she just meekly smiled. "You look tired," the woman continued and observed. "And you also look hungry." She took an apple out of a small bag and gave it to Hana. "Be careful. Take care and don't worry, everything will be all right from now on," said the old woman, who at that moment reminded Hana of a magical godmother from a fairy tale.

Hana bit into the apple. It was sweet and delicious. She believed it was the greatest delicacy in the world. She confidently got up and continued down the street to the Aschermanns'. But her nervousness returned as she neared her destination. It was Uncle Arthur who sent packages to Terezin with food, soap, toothpaste, gloves, or warm socks when he could. But what if they weren't at home? Or what if they were also deported before the end of the war? The questions were relentless. But then she also wondered if she might be united with her mother, father, and brother.

Would she?

Chapter 18

Meeting with Petr

Hana was woken from her daydreaming and speculation by the sharp sound of a siren from the fire engines rushing toward the Old Town Hall, from which smoke was still rising. She looked around, seeing and hearing laughing people waving Czechoslovakian flags, hugging each other, dancing and cheering. They were drowning in elation. Hana hadn't seen such collective happiness in a very long time. She did not realize that today was the official end of the Second World War in Europe after almost six years.

The Aschermanns' apartment was in a house almost at the end of the street near the Old-New Synagogue in the Jewish town section of Prague. Hana was anxiously approaching one of the most beautiful buildings on a glitzy Prague avenue. Uncle Arthur, as she called him, was actually her mother's uncle. Arthur was a successful and well-known general practitioner in Prague. Among many of his prominent patients were Germans who lived in the city. He was also a team physician for the well-known Czech soccer club of Slavia Prague. His wife Anna was called Aunt Anda. Her maiden name was Jirkovska, and she was an Aryan, which may be one of the reasons that Uncle Arthur was saved from deportation. Aunt Anda came from an upper-class Prague family and cared about proper manners.

Most people remembered the first Republic and were still practicing the traditional etiquette. In 1957, I remember visiting Aunt Anda not long after Uncle Arthur died. I was with my parents in the exact apartment my mother returned to after leaving the Terezin Ghetto. Several days prior to our visit, my mother gave me a lecture on correct behavior for such classy company. I was wearing a tie, which I never wore before. She almost made me feel uncomfortable. Even before entering their front door, my mother told me I had to greet Aunt Anda with the words "Kissing your hand, Auntie." Aunt Anda was an adamant stickler for it. It was Uncle Arthur who, through an intermediary and perhaps more intermediaries, sent medicine to the Kleins in the Terezin Ghetto. In taking such action he exhibited great courage. If it had been discovered, severe punishment would have followed—the whole family was at risk.

After the escape from Terezin, Hana stood in front of the colorful arch over the front door, raised her head, and took a moment to examine the decorative entrance as she had done many times before the occupation. This time, the door seemed smaller; she couldn't really figure out why it felt that way. She peeked through the small window into the interior, which she wasn't tall enough to be able to reach before the war: everything there was just as she remembered it, including the porcelain floor-mosaic in the hallway that she had liked as a little girl. She took a deep breath. She was feeling such uneasiness. She just held out her finger for a moment and then quickly withdrew her hand again. But then she rang the bell. Her heart was racing. It had been well over seven years since she had last stood here as a young, naive girl. She thought she could hear every beat of her heart now. Who would open the door, she wondered? Where would she go if no one answered? Her mind also pivoted again to her parents and brother, who had been deported from Terezin eight months earlier. How it had flown by! Were they alive? Were they okay?

But by then, the door was slowly opening. She froze. Her cousin Mancina opened the door, and their eyes met; both sets seemed to twinkle. Mancina's hands shot up in excitement. "Hanka, Hanka!" she shouted excitedly. "Is that you? Is it really you?" The girls fell into each other's arms. They squeezed each other for a long while with all their might. They began jumping around in circles with excitement. "Let me see what you look like," said Mancina after a moment. She stepped back a little from Hana and looked her over from head to toe. "What a big lady you are!" she smiled. Even the old woman at the church had recognized her as a young lady only moments ago.

But Hana knew very well that after three years of the Terezin Ghetto "cure" that she must be looking terrible. However, that didn't matter at this moment. Her nervousness left her—she was at home. The girls took each other's hands and walked together up the stairs to the apartment. Hana was again overtaken with a cautious anxiety about what awaited her in the next few moments. Who would be there?

For the next few moments, there was just pure joy. Before she knew it, Hana was already being lovingly smothered by Uncle Arthur and then by Aunt Anda. Everyone was laughing, stroking Hana's hair; the first tears of happiness appeared. But then Hana broke the spell and ventured to ask, "Do you know where my parents are? And Petr? Didn't they come to see you too?"

For a fraction of a second, they all fell silent, looking at each other, and then Mancina said, "Yes, Petr arrived at the end of April. He is out and about for a while. But your parents haven't arrived yet." She tried to emphasize the word "yet." And immediately she added, "I'm sure they'll be here soon!"

Auntie invited Hana to the table and asked her what she wanted to eat. Hana was taken aback with the opportunity to exercise her freedom; she hadn't had a choice in three years. She always ate what was there, or rather, what wasn't there. She just smiled and blinked rapidly at Aunt Anda, who knew immediately what was going on because she had experienced the same reaction with Petr several weeks prior. She brought something to eat and a glass of water to Hana, and then asked her if she wanted to take a bath. I must be really smelling horrible, Hana was thinking to herself. No matter what, that offer was heavenly music to Hana. A bathtub full of hot water? Just for her? She couldn't remember when she had had a real bath. In Terezin, water for washing was not always guaranteed. The girls took showers only occasionally, and even then, the water was just lukewarm. Often, they had to tolerate cold water in a cold environment, so she often returned to her room thoroughly chilled and shivering. But hygiene meant so much to Hana—a connection to the normal world. Mancina went to the bathroom to prepare a bath, then handed her a large towel and clean clothes from her own wardrobe. Hana disappeared into the bathroom. An hour passed, and she still hadn't emerged. Mancina took the door handle and cautiously peeked into the bathroom, but Hana wasn't there. Mancina went very quietly into the other rooms to check. She found Hana in one of the bedrooms, soundly asleep.

It was beginning to get dark outside when Petr returned. He was excitedly sharing with everyone the eventful celebration in the city. He was unstoppable in recounting everything he had experienced, until Mancina couldn't stand it and jumped in to announce,

"Hanka is here!" She hadn't even taken a breath to continue when Petr jumped out of his chair.

"What?" he shouted. "She is alive. Is she here? Is she okay? Where is she?" He was stuttering from the excitement. He started maniacally opening doors to rooms.

"Petr, calm down. Hanka is asleep, let her rest," Aunt Anda persuaded him.

Then Petr paused, content and believing that his sister was indeed there. He sat down again and began telling the details of his story that he had not shared with anyone yet. He believed now would be an appropriate time. "When I left on the transport to Auschwitz last October, I thought our parents and Hanka would soon follow. But when I remember what was happening there . . ." he paused for a moment, and tears appeared in his eyes. He lowered his head. The past was still too raw for him. The real hell on earth: Auschwitz. It would take him a long time to come to terms with it . . . if ever. So much suffering. So many dead. Death was everywhere. "There were so many prisoners, thousands. Only some managed to get news of their relatives. Only with extreme luck were you able to see your relatives if they arrived later or were already there before you. Mostly impossible," he paused again for a moment.

Then he lifted his head, and his tone turned, and he was more hopeful. "So, Hanka is here! That's wonderful!" He could not stand to wait. He sprang up and opened the door to the room where Hana was sleeping. His eyes had to see her, if only for a second. She was huddled in the covers, only her head peeking out. To Petr, it was like viewing the face of an angel, and it was enough to satisfy him, for that moment.

Hana didn't wake up; she slept all night. In the morning, everyone was sitting at the table eating breakfast when she, still looking sleepy, came out of the bedroom. But as soon as she saw Petr, she immediately went to him and collapsed into his arms. She could not believe he was real. They gripped each other, unable to speak. Spontaneous tears ran down their cheeks. It was a long time before they calmed down and were able to finally sit at the table. They felt it was their happiest day since they first left Prague.

Aunt Anda put a plate of food in front of Hana. This environment was still so surreal to her. But she didn't start eating right away, even though her stomach was growling. She wanted to enjoy the moment. Her co-prisoners of Room 29 would talk late at night about moments like this . . . dreaming aloud, they would be extremely tired, hungry, cold, bitten by lice. But the talks always helped them to feel slightly better. Their coping strategy. But now it was truly reality. The dream wasn't just a dream. This was actually happening. However, one major part of the dream was still missing—her parents and her husband.

Here she was, bathed, alert from a good night's sleep in a real bed, surrounded by her brother and other relatives, and such a feast in front of her. Anda urged Hana to start eating, but Petr understood what his sister was going through. He had been through it too. After a while, Hana finally started to eat. Slowly. She savored every bite. Ham, cheese, eggs, pickles, jam, fresh bread, and even real butter and cakes. Hana's eyes became watery again from the disbelief she felt. Is this really true? Only yesterday she was in Terezin; now she was in a normal Prague apartment with a bathtub, a soft bed with real feathers, clean clothes, delicacies on the table, cutlery, and colored porcelain plates. And, of course, her brother. Mancina asked Hana if she wanted a cup of coffee, but Hana asked instead for a glass of milk. She drank deeply until she had a white mustache above her lips.

Mancina and her parents wanted to ask Hana so much, but they remained quiet. They didn't want to touch the still-open wound. They also knew that Hana and Petr were primarily interested in what had happened to their parents.

It was a question no one wanted to broach, let alone answer.

Chapter 19

The Waiting Time

Early the next morning, Hana was still asleep when Petr left the apartment. He wanted to witness more history unfolding in Prague—the end of the war. These were dramatic times. Since he arrived at his aunt and uncle's apartment, he was drawn to the streets to immerse himself in and savor every triumphant event, every emotion in the heart of Prague. He had a strange feeling when he saw frightened and humiliated Germans somewhere. It was a great satisfaction for him.

At the corner of Celetna Street and Old Town Square, Petr met his friend Ota Sonnenschein Slunsky, whom he had met in the camp. When he arrived in Auschwitz at the beginning of October 1944, after a grueling journey of several days on a crowded cattle-car train, Petr was extremely lucky. Unlike most of his fellow passengers, he was not immediately sent to the gas chamber. Petr was young and still relatively strong, and the Nazis wanted to use him for work. He did not stay in Auschwitz for long. After his arrival there, he realized he was in real hell, where human life had lost its last vestiges of dignity.

At the end of 1944, months after arriving at Auschwitz, he was sent on a transport along with another group of young men to a forced labor camp in Meuselwitz, near Leipzig, a branch camp of Buchenwald concentration camp. It was built in 1944 in close proximity to HASAG factories manufacturing small- and medium-sized ammunition. HASAG (also known as Hugo Schneider AG, or by its original name in German: Hugo Schneider Aktiengesellschaft Metallwarenfabrik) was a German metal goods manufacturer founded in 1863. It was closed in 1947. As the Allied forces approached, evacuation transports began leaving the camp in early April 1945. Petr and his new acquaintance, Ota, were in one of them. In Kraslice, a town in Czechoslovakia near the German border, the train was attacked by Allied airplanes and heavily damaged. Many prisoners died, but a good number succeeded in escaping, and, in a miserable state, they managed to walk the approximately one hundred miles to Prague.

Petr and Ota, together with other people, embraced the jubilation over the end of the war and the feeling of freedom in the streets of Prague. When they came across a group of captured German soldiers, Petr bitterly thought to himself, "You wanted to destroy us all, but look, here we are again. And we are alive!" They both arrived at one of the barricades that were built during the Prague Uprising, which were no longer needed. Petr and Ota watched as men, women, and children dismantled the barricade again. They were removing paving stones, rubbish bins, wooden boxes, and all sorts of other objects that had served as an improvised barrier against the German soldiers. When Petr returned to the front of the house where the Aschermanns lived, he saw Hana walking introspectively along the sidewalk. He knew immediately that something was bothering her. He knew it wasn't physical. Something was tormenting her soul and giving her no peace, a feeling he understood so well. It was also clear to him his younger sister was going to have a much harder time dealing with the effects of trauma than he would. He tried to soothe her, but he wasn't very successful. He understood that what Hana needed above all was time.

His own thoughts often returned to Terezin, Auschwitz, and the armaments factories where, at the end of the war, he had to spend long hours day after day making munitions for the failing Third Reich. The painful memories were still too fresh. How could he make them go away? And was it worth thinking about the future? Brother and sister walked toward the Vltava River, passed by the still undemolished barracks, came to the Cechov Bridge, sat on a bench, and looked at the slowly flowing river with its small waves. Hana had already talked to Petr about nearly everything possible after the reunion, but she had not yet gotten to the most important subject: the fate of her parents. They had both avoided it.

Hana listened again to Petr's story of how he had escaped from the evacuation train at the Czech-German border and how he had traveled to Prague. When he paused for a moment, she turned her head toward him and smiled hesitantly with a soft, unexpected giggle. "Why are you laughing?" he asked her.

"Please don't take this the wrong way, but I actually escaped too—from Terezin," she told him, and proceeded to detail her trepidatious account.

"We were both lucky to get here safely," said Petr. He reminded her that they should register with the Czech authorities as soon as possible.

Hana smiled again. "I want to do it on May 12th."

"Why the 12th?" Peter asked.

"Don't you remember? It was May 12, 1942, when we all went to Terezin. It will be exactly three years," said Hana, her voice faltering again and tears appearing in her eyes. She leaned her head back against Petr's shoulder. They were suspended like that for a while in silence. Then they got up and slowly walked back to their new home.

Again, the fate of their parents went unaddressed.

At the Aschermans', Hana shared a bedroom with Petr. She went to bed early, wanting to sleep away all the black thoughts and memories, and she still felt exhausted. Petr soon followed her. But they couldn't truly fall asleep, rolling over from side to side. They engaged in all sorts of tapping and bending of pillows and blankets, but even so they could not settle. They just lay there for a while, only to repeat the rolling.

Finally, Petr whispered to Hana, "Are you asleep?" He didn't even wait for an answer and continued excitedly, "Do you have any idea where our parents might be? Do you know what happened?" He felt a little relieved at that moment. It was finally out in the open.

Hana quickly sat up in the bed and, with a raised voice, snapped at Peter, "You don't know? Please tell me that you know and that you know they'll be back soon . . ."

In the silent bedroom, Peter then heard Hana's sobs. He didn't know what to say; he wanted to avoid upsetting and hurting Hana even more. And, so, he offered only generalities, assuring her that their parents would certainly both come back in good time. But Hana hesitated to believe it. She had a dark feeling. She trembled and wept silently. "They both left Terezin October 10, 1944," she said in a firm voice that reflected that this date would never fade from her memory. "About two weeks after you," she continued. "Didn't you know that? I thought you met there."

This time even Peter lost his outward calm for a moment, his heart pounding like a drum inside. "No, I didn't know they were deported to Auschwitz. I hoped they would spend the rest of the war in Terezin . . ." He paused for a moment, then continued, "Almost every day, new trains arrived, thousands of prisoners, some had already arrived dead. It was impossible to find out who had arrived, let alone find relatives among them. Sometimes someone did manage to find them, but that was more of a coincidence."

Petr then told Hana a story about a time when a kapo, a guard from among the prisoners, told him that his Hana had come to Auschwitz and was hungry, but that he could give her food if Petr sent her something. "I didn't hesitate, even from the little we were given. I gave him part of the portion. It wasn't until I met you that I knew he was lying, that he had led me on to get my bread," Petr said resignedly and with frustration.

From Hana's account, however, he understood that he was still in Auschwitz when their parents arrived in a packed cattle truck. But what happened to them next? Neither he nor Hana wanted to think about the worst: the gas chambers. But he remembered very well the heavy black smoke that rose day and night from the chimneys of the crematoria, and the ever-present smell of burning human bodies. But there was no use deepening the pain they both felt inside. Above all, he told her they mustn't stop hoping that Mother and Father will come back! Maybe they're sick and couldn't come yet? Hana seemed too overcome by fatigue and began to fall asleep under the covers.

Petr said softly, "The Czech Red Cross is setting up an information center, so we can find out where the survivors are. And they will also read the names on the radio."

He covered his head with a pillow and tried to sleep as thoughts of his past haunted his dreams.

Chapter 20

In Search of the Future

Hana and Petr went to the police headquarters to apply for residency on Monday, May 14. This was necessary for those who may have moved before the war and served as a resource for anyone trying to locate those who may have survived or who had been displaced. Hana had done what she had set out to do—she had communicated the date of registration as May 12, the three-year anniversary of the transport to Terezin. She was sure that she would never forget these two dates: May 12, 1942, and May 12, 1945. But she wanted to forget the years in between, which she was unable to do, despite burying the memories in the most far-reaching corners of her mind.

She was knew how fortunate she was to have been able to live among her peers in Terezin, that she had made many friends among them, and that they had helped each other as much as they could. With some survivors, life became a little easier, with some it was a little more difficult. And some lived to see the end of the war, others did not. Thanks to the girls she met in the ghetto, Hana learned that one does not live only for oneself; she carried them all in her heart forever. In Terezin she grew up early and developed strong values in life that she might not have acquired under normal circumstances.

All the leaders in the L410 barrack who were in charge of the young girls helped Hana grow and remain ruthlessly resilient, even though at the time, no one knew in advance which among them would eventually end up on a transport to Auschwitz or another concentration camp. The leaders were all doing their best under the unbearable circumstances to prepare their pupils for life after liberation. It was in the misery of the Terezin Ghetto, or rather in the "oasis" of barrack L410, that the development of Hana's extraordinary character took shape. The relevant traits of survivorship she was forced to learn later helped her to overcome the other personal hardships of post-war life. And her compassionate conviction to help anyone who needed it was fostered there.

Hana was now only seventeen years old, living with her brother Petr and relatives in the center of Prague. She was well aware that this was not her permanent home. But where and what was a real home? What was her future? Her thoughts turned again to her parents. She sighed. If they were here, surely, they would know what to do next. She remembered the carefree days before the war, how she had run into her father's or mother's arms, with every ache in her body and soul, for comfort. Even in the ghetto she could rely on them; they were never very far.

Hana survived and was free. But was this really freedom? Every day she tried to cope with her new reality. She was managing a little more each day. There was plenty of food at the Aschermann house, regardless of the miserable supply situation in the city. Uncle Arthur was well connected as a doctor, and cousin Mancina provided her with clothing and helped her with anything she needed. But Hana tried to be as self-sufficient as possible. She didn't want to be a burden to anyone, but she could not yet be fully independent in the days of early recovery from the war. She remembered how her father always used to say to her, "The way you make your bed, that's how you lie down in it!" Both Hana and Petr received food and clothing vouchers from the Jewish organization and had a medical check-up. They both welcomed it, because it lessened their feeling of dependency on their uncle's family.

Hana was generally content, although the strong emotional impact of living in the Terezin Ghetto would affect her in sudden waves of depression. The first joyful days of her return seemed more and more often to be slipping into the darkness of the past. It was impossible to stop. She noticed that her brother was much better emotionally equipped to deal with overcoming their horrific history and could handle seemingly difficult situations of the present better than she could. She guessed that maybe men could cope with the traumas of the past better than women. The fact that he was older than she undoubtedly helped. While she was in the ghetto, the full impact of how many of her relatives and friends were dead was something she could not confront. But these truths faced her now, and they were impossible to turn away from. And more and more she realized that her parents might not come back at all. However, at the same time, her newly-charged optimism was manifesting itself: a determination to do her best to show everyone around that her survival was meaningful, that she deserved life.

She thought intensely about what to do next with her life. First and foremost, she must finish her education. This was her priority. Once things calmed down, she would start school again, and then everything else would develop from there. Walking along the Vltava River and around town was helpful for Hana to sort out her thoughts. She became her own counselor. One of her options she was considering was the music conservatory, as her friend Norbert Fryd had recommended in Terezin. He saw her in various performances there, and recognized she really enjoyed classical music. Fryd was a prominent person and prisoner in Terezin. Later he was deported to Auschwitz, which he survived and returned to Prague. Hana decided to give this music path some more thought.

During one of her walks, Hana noticed a group of people clearing debris from the barricades that were created in one of the streets. She immediately joined in and even smiled for a second. She realized that she had done almost nothing but physical labor for the last three years, and now, strangely enough, she was beginning to miss it. The women, of whom there were many, were talking amongst themselves about what they had done during the war—it became apparent they didn't know each other. For obvious reasons, Hana refrained from speaking about her past. When it was her implied turn, she lied, even though her parents had told her since childhood that she must not lie. "During the war, we were on my grandparents' farm, not too far from Prague, and now I am here visiting my uncle." The women accepted it. No one could tell she was lying. No one probably cared. It was the first time she refused to talk about her past to anyone. She realized that in the future, she would probably get questions like this often, but she didn't want to discuss being in Terezin and what she had experienced there. She was convinced that many people would not believe or understand her anyway. She then went to work on the street every day. This helped her to repress any thoughts of the ghetto and of her parents. She arranged with Petr that he would check the daily lists of survivors . . . perhaps . . . .

One afternoon, Hana wanted to rest after a long walk, and she sat down at the Jan Hus memorial in Old Town Square. Two girls her age were walking by. In one of them she recognized her cellmate from the Terezin barrack L410, and the other she did not know. She was about to jump up and run after them, but some unknown force held her in place. It was an awkward and uncomfortable moment. Her heart thumped. She suddenly wasn't sure she wanted to meet her former roommate. She felt she wasn't ready to cast her mind back to the terrors of the ghetto she had only recently left. She was too vulnerable. After a while of avoidance, Hana got up and went to help clear away the street debris that still remained as a memory of the war.

Hana asked Petr every day if he had learned anything new about their parents, but the answer was always the same, "No, unfortunately, but they say it doesn't mean anything for certain yet." Petr was regularly told in the office that for survivors it can take a long time to return home. Hope was still alive. And Petr tried to reassure his younger sister with similar sentiment.

Days and weeks passed. Still no news of their parents. Even Petr didn't believe much anymore that their mother and father would come back, but he didn't show it outwardly in front of his sister. One day he even learned that, with a few exceptions, everyone on the transport that included his parents had gone straight to the gas chamber. Petr certainly had no plans to share such news with Hana, even though he knew that the longer it took, the less likely it was that they would return. He left for home in a very melancholy mood, almost certain that he would never see his parents again. The resurfacing memories of his arrival in Auschwitz and the ignominious selection process that decided life and death were replaying in his mind. He was convinced that his parents were no longer alive.

Years ago, when I was researching my mother's fate, I received an email from New York from Martha Druckerova-Cornell, who had lived with my mother in Room 29 in Terezin. She wrote to me saying that she knew Hana's mother, Marta, had died a few months after she and her husband, Rudolf, arrived in Auschwitz from Terezin. Initially, Marta was selected for work but later died on the death march. But Martha could not substantiate this in any way. I didn't take it too seriously, because I was convinced that my grandparents had died immediately after arriving in Auschwitz, as was suggested by the Auschwitz archives, probably on October 19, 1944. The email from them cited that all of the last transports of prisoners arriving from Terezin were sent directly to the gas chambers. No recording of names. The Nazis were in a hurry.

But then a transcribed interview with Martha Zenkerova-Bloch that she had granted her daughter Ellen in the late 1980s came into my hands. Martha and my mother were cousins. My mother's father, Rudolf, and Martha's mother, Hermina, were siblings. Martha spent several years in the Terezin Ghetto and was later transported to Auschwitz. In that interview, she asked her daughter, Ellen, "Do you remember Hana Kleinova-Fristenska? We met her in Switzerland." Ellen nodded in agreement. "Her mother, Marta, was with me in Terezin and then in Auschwitz. She didn't go to the gas chambers. We lived together in one of the large wooden barracks. We were working; however, she was my guardian angel. I was sick, and she brought me food and even gave me some of her portion. Imagine that. We were all very hungry, and she gave me some of her own. No one could do that but an angel. By the time we were on the death march, I was so exhausted I couldn't go on anymore. And Hanka's mother said to me then, 'I have to go on, I have two children.'"

Ellen asked her mother what happened to Marta, if she had died on the march. "Who knows?" Martha replied, and then added, "I guess no one will ever know. As she slowly walked away, I managed to tell her, 'You're right, you have to keep going because you have children.' But I'll never forget her giving me half of her food. She always brought it to me."

How things actually unfolded with my grandparents Marta and Rudolf, I'll never know. Even Hana and Petr had no idea, even though they already knew the truth that their parents would not return. They held each other for a long time and cried. Hana felt that the world was ending, that nothing was worth it anymore. Petr comforted and encouraged her, "They would have wanted us to go on, not give up." Hana would tell herself that over and over again, and that she needed to be even stronger now.

One Sunday, Petr suggested to Hana that they go for a walk together to the Stromovka Park. It was a nice, warm day. They took the tram, and Hana's heart clenched as she recognized the places where her journey to Terezin had begun four years earlier. Petr apparently realized it too. The two siblings stared into each other's eyes for a moment. Nothing more needed to be said. In the park, there were quite a few people, and they walked in silence for a long while, when Hana thought this was now the appropriate time to talk about their future. She was about to speak when Petr initiated the conversation.

"Hanka," he said to her in a serious tone, taking a deep breath. He obviously had something important to tell his sister. "You know," he continued, "I'm . . . I'm really thinking about joining the army. I've talked to a few people in the Jewish community, and some of the guys my age are thinking about it too." And it was out.

Hana stopped and looked into her brother's eyes. "Why?" she asked. She couldn't believe it. After everything she had experienced in Terezin, after what the war had done. "Why the army? Haven't you had enough of soldiers?" she posed to him. Petr tried to explain to her that this was a completely different army, a different situation. Besides, he could make quite a career there where he would have a guaranteed income and other benefits. And he would do what he liked: a new military school for aircraft mechanics was just opening near Liberec.

After a moment, Hana realized that Petr had already made up his mind about his future. And she even found herself a little envious of him because he knew what he wanted to do next. She understood that soon they would each be on their own. Her twenty-year-old brother was going to be a soldier. In the end, she wanted to be supportive. Hana knew that her time for a major life change would also come, and it would happen sooner than she expected.

A few weeks later, on a June day, returning from a walk, she ran into Hanus Sladky, whose wife, Hilda, had promised Hana's mother in Terezin that she would take care of her. Hana was overjoyed, and she hugged him with sincere gratitude. "Is Hilda here too?" Hana asked, looking around.

"No, she's not here, I'm sorry," Hanus told her. He explained that he was in Prague for a few days to take care of some family business, and Hilda was staying at home in Zabreh in Moravia. They sat down on a bench and recounted to each other how they got out of Terezin and what they had been doing since they had last seen each other. Hanus told Hana that Hilda's father Gustav Taussig had owned a pottery workshop in Zabreh before the war, which he, Hilda, and her brother Rudolf now wanted to reopen. He told Hana how Hilda's painful memories of the ghetto came back to her and that working on the rebuilding of the workshop was a pleasant diversion. His wife would certainly be extremely pleased to see Hana again.

Hana confided in Hanus that she, too, was struggling with her Terezin demons, that her parents were presumably dead, that her brother Petr was leaving her to serve in the newly formed Czechoslovakian army, and that she was now living with relatives where she did not feel at home. Some weight had now been lifted from her in being able to confide in Hanus. Although again, it was not without tears. "You know, my aunt and uncle are very good to me. They've never had a harsh word for me or have even shown somehow that I would be bothering them, but I don't feel very comfortable there. I feel like I don't belong there," Hana said.

Hanus then said something that took Hana by surprise, and it completely changed her life. He invited her to move in with them at their house in Zabreh.

Hanus later recalled this in his memoirs in a Terezin collection, which my friend Pavel Taussig pointed out to me. He wrote, "It was sometime in July of 1945, Hanka and I met by accident in Prague, just like it sometimes happened in Terezin. It was in Parizska Street. I asked how she was doing, and she told me with tears in her eyes that her parents had not returned and that she was living with relatives. She feels like a burden and doesn't know what to do. We lived in Zabreh in Moravia, where we got back the business and the house of Hilda's parents. We had enough space in the house, so I invited Hanka to move to Zabreh and live with us. There was a business school in the neighboring town of Sumperk, and Hilda's brother Rudolf Taussig knew the headmaster well. One phone call was all it took for Hanka to begin school."

And so the Sladky family grew by an adopted daughter.

Chapter 21

Back in School

It was the end of August 1945, and Hilda was waiting at the train station in Zabreh na Morave. The train arrived on time, and she was straining her neck looking for Hana. There she was! She gained some weight but had the same smile, Hilda thought. When Hana saw Hilda, her pulse danced with joy, she hurried her stride, and then she ended up in the long, sincere embrace of her second mother from Terezin. Both of them could not stop their tears of happiness, nor did they wish to. After most of the passengers left the platform, the two women were still holding each other. Hilda finally whispered in Hana's ear, "Well, I guess we'd better be going, we won't miss anything. We'll have plenty of time to ourselves."

Hana only had a small suitcase and a backpack. The doting mother figure wanted to help Hana, but she respected her wishes to carry the luggage herself. "Suit yourself," Hilda told her, smiling. "Anyway, our house is just a block away from here." There was no room for silence on the short trip to Hilda's. They each wanted to tell the other every detail of everything they had experienced since they had been separated in May 1945. It didn't take long before they were standing at the gate of the Taussigs' house on Nadrazni Street. It was actually two buildings, with a red brick building behind the family home. Later, Hana learned that the secondary building was the pottery workshop Hanus had mentioned while they were in Prague.

Hilda first took Hana to the rather large kitchen to eat after the long journey. Then she took her to her new room in the attic of the house. Hana looked around the room and suddenly realized that after a few years she would have a room all to herself again. She was left alone for a moment to put her personal belongings away, and in no time the few items that she had brought with her were organized. Then she sighed deeply with some fulfillment and stretched out on the bed for a moment to get some rest.

Although it was an unfamiliar environment for her, she felt much more comfortable here than in Prague while with the Aschermanns. Hilda's presence filled her with happiness and contentment, and she was finally sure that she would be at ease here. As she lay on the bed and stared at the ceiling, memories of Terezin came back to her for a brief moment, but knowing she could stretch out on this bed and relax was now reassuring, and images of Terezin melted away. She wanted to believe that in her new surroundings, next to Hilda, thoughts of the ghetto might disappear forever. She believed that it would help her to return to a new normal life. Hana was overwhelmed by a feeling of satisfaction, a small but significant milestone of happiness . . . the kind she used to have with her mother and father. But that was before the war . . . .

That same weekend, Hilda's brother Rudolf Taussig arrived. Shortly before the outbreak of the war, he had gone to England via Palestine, where he served in the Czechoslovakian army that was based in England. He was even the personal driver of General Alois Liska, commander of a separate armored brigade. At that time, he was finishing his military service near Zabreh. Hana took an instant liking to him. Since Rudolf knew the director of the Business Academy in Sumperk personally, he and Hanus discussed the possibility of Hana studying there. Rudolf brought the proposal up to her, and she gladly accepted it.

The very next day, Hana and Hilda went to Sumperk to see everything and get more information. They talked with the school's director about the specifics and had to take some paperwork back home. For about one month, the classes were already in session, but that didn't seem to be an issue. However, Hana was slightly concerned that she really officially had not been in regular school for the last five years. This might be a challenging adjustment for her.

When they were on the train back home, Hilda asked how Hana felt about the school. "Daddy was a great businessman, so maybe I have some of his brain cells," smiled Hana, "I find all the subjects useful, but I still have to think it all through." She mentioned to Hilda her apprehension about the long break from school.

Hilda answered with a subtle grin, "I know you. You will study twice as hard as your future classmates, so I am not worried about it at all." Hana felt much better because she knew that Hilda would fully support her. That evening, she fell soundly asleep. The idea of starting school again was a growing thrill to her. She began to look forward to it.

Rudolf Taussig obviously was well-connected in Sumperk, and Hana could start school immediately. Hana had much catching up to do, but she enjoyed learning and was hungry for education. She commuted to school every day by train and had to get up very early but didn't mind. Of course, she was used to a regular routine with early wake-up calls. One of her classmates, Svatava, also commuted by the same train. She lived in the village of Hrabova near Zabreh, so they traveled to school together, which made the journey time pass more quickly. Sometimes they even studied together when Svatava invited Hana to her house. They met a few more times after 1990. (While conducting my research for this book, I didn't know about Svatava's role in my mother's life. Unfortunately, when I wanted to interview her, she had already passed away.)

When Hana didn't have to study, which wasn't very often, she spent all her free time with Hilda. There exist photos from that time period, and my mother was in many pictures with Hilda. She looked very happy with genuine smiles. One would never know she had ever experienced all the hardships of the Terezin Ghetto; she had somehow managed to cut herself off from that past. Now she was with Hilda, in the safety and support of the Taussig family, and in a new school. The outlook could not have been more hopeful. Hana and Hilda used their free time for long walks, sometimes as far as the city limits and beyond. On weekends, when Rudolf came home, he sometimes took them on trips by car somewhere further out of town. Hana, with Hilda by her side, explored the beauty of the surrounding countryside, and she occasionally reminisced about the pre-war trips with her family.

Hilda regularly asked her if she was doing well at school, if she needed help with anything. "You can ask me for anything. I'll help you every time," Hilda told her honestly. Hana beamed and looked into her friend's eyes.

"Thank you, thank you so much, for everything. I'll never forget it," said Hana, patting Hilda on the shoulder. She confided that everyone at school was helping her, going out of their way to help her. "You know, I have the most trouble with simple merchant's arithmetic and bookkeeping," she said to Hilda. "This is all Greek to me. I don't think I know how to count and calculate," laughed Hana. "Luckily, Svatava is very good at it and is tutoring me."

Time passed quickly. Suddenly, Christmas was upon them, the first since the country had been liberated. Hana enjoyed it very much. (I wasn't able to find out if the Klein family celebrated Christmas or not. When growing up, my family always celebrated traditional Christmas.) Under the tree Hana found some clothes and a few practical things for a young lady. These were truly joyful moments. At the end of January 1946, Rudolf finally returned; his army duty was definitely over. Hana tried to help in the household as much as she could. She wanted to show how much she appreciated being with them.

One day, Hilda confided to Hana that she was expecting an addition to the family in August; she was pregnant! Hana was sincerely glad for her. However, the memory of Terezin resurfaced in her mind and could not be repressed. She thought of her Terezin husband, who had left on the transport to unknown places, and of their child, who never had the opportunity to live. But she certainly didn't want to talk about it with anyone. She acknowledged to Hilda that she had noticed her larger tummy, but she didn't want to be too curious and had waited for her to share the news. Hana was looking forward to being a nanny.

Now that Rudolf was still at home, the three of them often went on trips together. Rudolf liked to drive; he was an excellent chauffeur. And he loved to see the two women enjoying their trips. In the summer, Hana received her first report card—she showed considerable achievement and was very happy and proud of how she had managed the challenges of the school year. She still corresponded with her brother Petr, who did not change his decision and joined the army. Petr was very happy that his sister was doing well in school and wrote to her to tell her how proud he was of her. Hana was even able to meet up with her brother on occasion at the Aschermanns' in Prague. Hilda and Hanus accompanied her. They all had much to talk about.

In Zabreh, Hana and Hilda continued their exploration of the near and distant surroundings. Alena Taussig, Rudolf's wife, shared a memory with me years later. The girls were out of town again, they returned home late, after dark, covered in dirt, their shoes and trousers dirty. When Rudolf asked them where they had been, they replied that they had been in the field, digging up beets and eating them right away. They said that the beets were smaller than those in the fields of Terezin, but much tastier. Rudolf told them that they were stealing other people's property and that they should be ashamed of themselves. Laughing, the girls replied that they were careful not to be seen and that they didn't view it that way. How terrible the food must have been in Terezin, since more than a year after the war, the beetroot straight from the ground was such a delicacy for them that they even risked being caught!

Then Alena told me one more story about how pretty my mother was. "One day I was in a store, standing in line. And then the door opened, and in walked Hilda and Hana, and everybody was staring at them. Since they didn't want to wait in line, Hilda called out to the clerk, Mr. Havlena, asking if they had one particular item. He replied that it hadn't arrived yet, so the two girls turned and disappeared outside. As soon as the door closed, several customers asked Mr. Havlena who the pretty girl with Hilda was. And he told them that she was Rudolf Taussig's fiancée, whom he had brought from abroad. If I had been in the shop longer, I would have corrected that statement to everyone to announce that I was actually Rudolf's fiancée." Rudolf and Alena often recalled the incident with laughter.

At the end of August, Hilda gave birth to a daughter, Zuzanka, a beautiful little girl. A child whose very existence was of great significance. She was born to parents who, according to the Final Solution to the Jewish Question, should have and would have been dead long ago. But they had survived, and now they had their longed-for child, who was a miraculous gift. Everyone was ecstatic about the birth of their child, including Hana, despite her still resonant sorrow over the loss of her own child during the dark days of Terezin.

Life finds a way.

Chapter 22

Rescue at the Right Moment

On the first day of school, after the summer break, Hana met her classmate Svatava at the train station in Zabreh, and together they boarded the train to Sumperk. Outside the window, the sunny countryside was floating by while Hana's reflections went back to the previous few months, beginning with her arrival in her new home in Zabreh, to meeting Hilda, who had become her closest friend, to her adventurous trips to the countryside, to, of course, the birth of Zuzana. Hana felt that after several years of suffering, her life was once again on a positive trajectory. Life was good. Moreover, she was going to school again, which she enjoyed very much. She was oblivious to the calamity the coming months and years would bring, the further turbulent changes her life would undergo.

But first things first. Under what circumstances my mother, Hana Kleinova, met my father, Jarek Fristensky, I never found out, although I asked every possible relative and acquaintance about it. It just happened. This can be said of many future lifelong meetings . . . they occur unplanned, by chance. Jarek as he was called, i.e., Jaromir Fristensky, was an early Christmas present, born on December 15, 1924, in Vendryne as the second son of Frantisek and Marie (Klestilova) Fristensky. The firstborn, Dalibor, was three years older. In 1922, Frantisek Fristensky, my grandfather (a formidable athlete who toured the USA twice in his career as a professional wrestler and brother of the well-known wrestler-athlete, Gustav), bought a large farm, a distillery, and a steam sawmill there in this village near the border to Poland in the east of Czechoslovakia.

In 1926, Frantisek sold everything and moved with his family to Luzice near Sternberk, where he and his brother Gustav leased a rather large farm, which Frantisek successfully managed and ran. This was also the birthplace of Jarek's other brothers, Zdenek and Gustav. After the Munich Agreement in the autumn of 1938, Luzice became part of the Sudetenland and consequently a portion of the German Reich. The Fristensky brothers lost all their property. All the Czech nationals had to clear the region. The elder Gustav continued to pursue his wrestling career, although on a smaller scale, and at the end of 1938, Frantisek bought a farm in Bedihost near Prostejov, where he, within sixteen years, started his third farming business.

Frantisek's sons were involved in the work on the farm, but besides that, the three of them also continued the sporting career of the Fristensky family, although not in wrestling. Jarek played soccer and ice hockey for the clubs of Bedihost. Zdenek also played ice hockey for Bedihost, and later, the youngest, Gustav, joined the older brothers. The oldest of the four brothers, Dalibor, moved to Prague and worked as an administrator.

The wartime was difficult for all of them. Jarek joined the Bata Shoe-Factory in Zlin, where he continued to play soccer. He once told me how the entire team, instead of practicing, watched the world-famous track star, Emil Zatopek, who was circling the athletic oval in heavy military boots. Zdenek and Gustav stayed in Bedihost and helped on the farm.

The Tenth Historical Stop

Gustav, the Wrestler, Against the Reich

Gustav Fristensky is still the most famous wrestler-athlete in Czech history. However, his resistance activities during the German occupation are less known. Author Bretislav Ditrych described these activities in detail in his book S pozdravem Sîlle zdar Gustav Fristensky *(Saluting the Strength of Gustav Fristensky). At the end of the summer of 1943, Gustav was visited in Litovel by a man named Adolf Cingros, an employee of the Olomouc insurance company Patria. He brought a confidential message from the members of the Revolutionary National Committee in Olomouc asking if Gustav would join the resistance. Gustav, who knew Cingros, agreed without hesitation. He felt it was his duty. Whenever and wherever the words "homeland" and "patriotism" came up, he never hesitated to help.*

On his next visit Cingros brought Gustav messages from retired policeman Major Jindrich, addressed to an officer Funek in the nearby town of Uncovice. And he asked for a monetary contribution to a resistance fund for the families of arrested and imprisoned men who had been involved in resistance activities. Gustav, himself, proposed to contribute ten thousand crowns a month.

However, before Christmas 1943, the Gestapo arrested retired Major Bombera (who was helping the resistance movement) for hiding weapons (he was later executed in January 1945) and began to follow Adolf Cingros as well. In February 1944, he visited Gustav again, but he did not say much and was obviously restless. He took the agreed amount from Gustav and soon left again. A few days later, Gustav went to Prague for a meeting about a planned wrestling competition. During his absence from his home in Litovel, three Gestapo men arrived and searched his house. They took a radio and two hunting rifles. On the same day, Gustav was arrested at the Neptun Hotel in Prague and imprisoned in the Petschek Palace, where the Gestapo was based.

"I stayed in the cell for long, grim hours without knowing why I was there. In one of the rooms, in a dim light, a Gestapo officer was motionlessly sitting behind a desk. Either he was lazily writing something down, smoking, or reading the newspaper, and in all sorts of ways shortening the long moments until his duty hour was up. For me, every hour was an eternity, staring dully and motionlessly at the gray wall not knowing what would happen next. Only occasionally there was some excitement when a new victim was brought in, or another was taken from our vicinity into the unknown . . ." described Gustav of the first moments after his arrest.

He was then transferred to Pankrac Prison, also in Prague, and a few days later to Olomouc, a town near Litovel. The Olomouc Gestapo prison was only a transfer facility. It was here that prisoners were in the hands of the Gestapo, interrogated before sent to trials, other prisons or directly to concentration camps. By then, of course, his wife Miroslava was looking for him, and she even ventured to Prague to locate him. But it was only after nine days that she received a short message from her husband from the Olomouc prison, asking for clean clothes. In vain, she tried to visit with her husband for even a little time. Everything was forbidden with the justification that Gustav refused to confess.

In the end, the attempt was successful, and the visit was described as follows by Gustav's niece Pavla Novotna, who went to the Olomouc prison with Miroslava Fristenska: "I accompanied her. The square visiting room was enclosed by iron bars, two chairs, and a table. They brought in my uncle. He was 65 years old, but I always knew him as a burly, sturdy man with a keen eye who walked upright. Now he came in thin, his convict clothes hanging off him. It was the first time I'd seen him with gray hair. We were horrified; my aunt cried . . . They shouted at him and at us; we were not able to hug each other, not even to shake hands."

Fristensky was known as a wrestler even by some guards and Germans. They threatened him during interrogation but never tried to hit him. Gustav kept denying everything. One night the guard opened the door and ordered Gustav to come out. He feared the worst. But he was only transferred to another cell with fourteen cellmates. After another ten days, Gustav was taken to Brno, where he was subjected to more and more interrogations. From there he traveled by train (accompanied by Gestapo guards) to the court in Wroclaw in Poland. Two days before the trial, Gustav wrote a letter on toilet paper to his wife Miroslava and asked the guard, who knew him from his pre-war athletic career in Hamburg, to put it in an envelope and send it to Litovel.

"I am sure that I have followed the right path in my life, that I have always made not only our people at home but also abroad happy with my good sportsmanship," Gustav wrote to his wife and gave her instructions on how to take care of his many prizes, archive, his Fiat car, horse harness, bicycle, photographs, and other personal belongings. "If I don't survive the war, then I'll be looking at all of you from the cloudy heights."

Then, it was as if a small miracle had happened. Although three men from the captured resistance group were sentenced to death and a fourth received two years in prison, Fristensky was freed. He may also have been helped by a letter from the Czechoslovakian Minister of the Interior, Richard Bienert, who wrote it at the request of Gustav's wife. A few days later, Gustav got off the train in Olomouc. But he did not get home yet, because he ended up in prison again. The head of the Olomouc Gestapo prison, SS-Hauptsturmführer Heinrich Gottschling, could not accept that Fristensky had left the court without punishment. He was put in the prison again for two days, and consequently, they decided to send him to the Mauthausen concentration camp. However, just after a few days of interrogation, he was to leave there back to Olomouc. His wife Miroslava found out that Gustav was back in the Olomouc prison, and rushed to Olomouc and was allowed to meet with her husband. Gustav remembered that during his first stay in the Olomouc prison, a fellow prisoner told him about a commander who might be bribed.

In the end, Miroslava Fristenska somehow managed to get to the prison commander, through whatever means it took. Three days later, Gustav was released. The Czech poet Petr Bezruc sent Miroslava a quatrain: "Thank you

Lord / for hearing my plea / so that Mr. Fristensky / came out of the evil prison
as free." How much did Miroslava end up paying to free her husband? She
never told him. "It was not until three years after her death that I found in her
small packet calendar a note that read – 'gold jewelry' and next to it 'Gestapo,'"
Gustav later confided. In addition to the golden pay-out, his wife added a large
sum of money she had saved. Immediately after his release from prison, Gustav
Fristensky helped those who remained in prison.

 When, after the war, the Minister of the Interior, Bienert, was tried in
Prague, Miroslava Fristenska sent a letter to his lawyer, reminding him that he
had contributed to her husband's liberation. Gustav also felt obliged to make the
same intervention, even though at the time it might have done him more harm.

In the autumn of 1945, my father, Jarek Fristensky, enrolled at the
State Industrial College of Electronics in Sumperk, where he moved
in early October. According to various indications, I estimate that
Jarek and Hana met sometime in the spring of 1947, when Hana
moved from Zabreh to Sumperk because of the commuting challenges. Perhaps they first met at a student party. Hana was a very
pretty, young woman, and I can imagine how men were attracted
to her. But I also think that after the tragically-ended friendships
and unfulfilled motherhood from Terezin, she didn't rush into any
serious relationships. Alena Taussig even attested that Hana avoided
forming any serious male friendships.

 Before Hana moved to Sumperk, in the autumn of 1946, she
devoted all her free time to Hilda. After Hilda gave birth, she did not
return to her original state of health, which worried everyone. I later
found in my mother's school report cards that she had many excused
hours of absence from school at that time. Undoubtedly because she
wanted to take care of Hilda. She surely knew well what it meant
for them to help each other. Hilda's health continued to decline,
and she even had to be taken to the hospital in Olomouc. Hilda's
nephew, Pavel, told me she may have suffered from some incurable
blood disease.

Hilda died on March 7, 1947, which was a cruel blow to Hana and the Taussig and Sladky families. They all understandably took it very hard. For Hana, it was another tragic setback in her life. A shock. A tragedy. The death of her best friend, and at some moments, almost like her second mother. Suddenly, she wasn't there. Why? Why did it happen? Hana's relationship and love for Hilda and the entire Taussig family is evidenced by the published death notice, which identifies her as a foster daughter. She became part of the family. Rudolf Taussig, who supported Hana, was the one who helped her the most during that time. He made the transition from Prague to Zabreh as comfortable for her as possible. He understood well what she had experienced during the previous two years.

Because of Hilda's death, Hana's world began to crumble again. She was cruelly robbed of yet another important person, and the weight it piled on her seemed insurmountable . . . just when her life seemed to be turning around. Suddenly, she felt alone again, abandoned, even though there were still people around her who helped her and whom she loved. But there was only one missing—Hilda. Without her, life was suddenly extremely difficult again. Hana couldn't cope. She decided to move to Sumperk. She could have stayed in Zabreh and commuted, but she needed a change, a new purpose in her life.

It was in this state of mind, in her grief after Hilda's death, that she met Jarek Fristensky. Was it indeed just a coincidence? Perhaps. But in this trying time for her, it was the best timing for Hana . . . destiny. "Nothing better could have happened to her at that time," Pavel Taussig, the son of Rudolf and Alena Taussig, once told me. It was as if Hana and Jarek were meant and chosen for each other. They fit together like two pieces of a puzzle. She was there for him, and he was there for her. A relationship for life. For better or worse. They were soulmates.

In 2017, I was in contact with Stella Brollova-Repper, who lived in Falls Church, Virginia. She was Hana's former roommate from the Terezin Ghetto. She told me that Hana, with the supportive approval of the Taussigs, invited her to Zabreh after the war. "I always got along well with Hanka in Terezin," Stella told me, when I met her at her American home. "After the liberation, I never expected that we would ever meet again. But we stayed in touch, and that's how I got to Zabreh and the Taussigs' ceramic workshop. In our free time we walked around the city and talked about the future. Hanka told me enthusiastically about Jarek Fristensky. He often came to visit her in Zabreh on his motorbike. She said he always put Hanka on the seat behind him and they were off together." When I asked Stella if they ever remembered and talked about their time in the Terezin Ghetto, she resolutely replied, "Never."

Many books have been written about the Fristensky family, and Gustav became a symbol of superhuman strength. I talked about this in 2016 in Israel with Maud Beer-Stecklemacher, who also lived with Hana in Terezin's L410 barrack. She told me that she came from Prostejov, a town about forty miles south of Zabreh. She told me, "It was common in the Czech lands to say that someone was strong like Fristensky. But his name was also used by parents when they wanted to scare their children: if you do not behave, we will send Fristensky after you; he will put you in line!"

In June 1947, Hana graduated from business school and joined a company in Sumperk as an office clerk. Her relationship with Jarek was noticeably flourishing. They saw each other as much as possible. They also visited the Taussigs in Zabreh together, and they went on motorcycle trips together. It must have been love at first sight. But Hana was still struggling internally with her past; she didn't want to be hurt and disappointed again. After Hilda's death, she no longer had anyone she could safely confide in, who understood and trusted her. "I think Jarek understood that very well. He didn't need to know every detail of Hana's past. What he knew was enough. He understood that Hana needed a careful approach, understanding, and respect. And Jarek succeeded in giving her that. He was the right person for Hanka at the right time," Pavel Taussig told me in one of our many talks.

Hana's final acceptance of her relationship with Jarek was gradual because of the ghosts of the past. But over time, she gave herself to him, fell in love with him. She was also impressed with his athleticism. At that time, Jarek, along with his brother Zdenek, was a well-established motorcycle racer, and she attended many races around the country with them. One time, Zdenek jokingly told me that I was almost born in the motorcycle depot.

Many of the girls from the L410 barracks and directly from Hana's Room 29 moved to Israel after the liberation. Ilona Steinova-Weinstock told me how she met with Hana after the war in Prague and offered her an invitation to emigrate with her and her sister, Ela, to the Middle East. "It was just before my sister, mother, and I left for Israel. She knew both of us well, so I believed it would be an easy decision for her. I tried to convince Hana to come with us as well. But she refused," Ilona told me. Why? "She couldn't leave her brother Petr, and above all, she already had a serious relationship with your dad."

And then, laughingly, Ilona told me, "If she had listened to us then and gone to Israel with us, you wouldn't be sitting here talking to me now. I didn't see your mother again until forty years later, when she came to visit me in New York, where I then moved from Israel. Your dad was with her then too. After meeting him, I think that she made the right decision."

Jarek was indeed the best thing that could have happened to Hana at just the right time.

Chapter 23

My Birth

February 1948 became one of the most tragic months of Czech, or rather Czechoslovakian history, since at that time, Czechs and Slovaks belonged to one country. The Communists came to power for 41 long years. But from my mother's personal point of view, it was actually a blissful month—she got pregnant. A new life thrived in her womb . . . me.

It wasn't completely unexpected; Hana and Jarek had been together every free moment in the last months. According to Pavel Taussig, my mother had claimed she never wanted to have children after her tragic experience in Terezin, but her relationship with Jarek Fristensky had completely transformed her original resolution. However, Jarek still had not found the appropriate time and manner to announce his relationship with Hana to his parents. They had not yet been together at the family farm residence in Bedihost. But Hana's pregnancy was about to change that, and Jarek believed that this was the ideal moment to introduce his girlfriend to his parents, and, at the same time, tell them that they were going to be a grandmother and grandfather.

Jarek thought his parents would be thrilled with the news, so he was caught off guard by their reaction of disapproval. His father told him emphatically that he did not wish for his son to bring Hana to Bedihost at all. When I learned this many years later from a story by Alena and Pavel Taussig, I didn't even want to believe it. My memories of my grandmother and grandfather, and their relationship with my mother, were always very pleasant. I never observed any hard feelings between my mother and her in-laws. She actually called them mother and father. It seemed to me that their relationship couldn't have been more sincere and loving. At one point, my mother told me, "Your father's mother was really like my mom to me; we were best friends. I learned what I know today in the kitchen and running the household from your grandmother in Bedihost. She couldn't have been nicer to me. And your grandfather," she continued, "he was strict but fair, a real hard worker. And when you were born, he became the grandfather he should have been. He helped me a lot, too, and when you were growing up, he often took you with him wherever he could."

What was the problem then? Why did my grandparents reject Hana at first? When I tried to get to the bottom of it and talked to several relatives and friends, the conclusion was that it most likely pointed to anti-Semitism. They were very guarded in discussing this subject with me. Hana was Jewish—that was the problem. Considering the immediate aftermath of the war, it may seem unbelievable, but anti-Semitism was quite deeply rooted in certain layers of Bohemian and Moravian nationalist society—even long before Hitler came to power.

There is much historical evidence to support this sentiment. For example, the so-called Hilsner Riot was a catalyst, and it prompted a period with the greatest manifestations of anti-Semitism during the 19th century in Czech territory.

During the war, anti-Semitism also appeared among officers and other soldiers in Czechoslovakian foreign armies. The tone did not disappear in post-war Czechoslovakia, which underwent significant ethnic homogenization. Hostile sentiments toward minorities had been developing there since the Munich crisis in the autumn of 1938, and prominent communist functionaries fed on it. Czechoslovakia was by no means alone in this, as strong anti-Semitism also prevailed in Poland. In Kielce, for example, a bloody anti-Jewish pogrom took place at the beginning of July 1946, which resulted in 42 deaths.

The Eleventh Historical Stop

"Entrance for Dogs and Jews is Forbidden"

Kurt Wehle spent several years in Terezin. When he returned to Prague after the liberation, the authorities provided him with an apartment. "That was a very ugly experience. You could hear the Czechs saying, 'Those Hitler gas chambers were somehow leaky, more Jews came back than left!' That was the atmosphere. People were indoctrinated by their own Czech fascists, and then by the Germans," he told the USC Shoah Foundation, which collected memories of survivors for educational programs years later. It was certainly not an isolated pattern. A Jewish young man, Kurt Gregor, a soldier in the Liberation Allied Army, visited the Sumava Mountains in Czechoslovakia after the war. And there was a sign hanging on a pub there that read, "No dogs or Jews allowed" in Czech and in German. After the occupation, the innkeeper took down only the German part of the sign. Nobody minded, no one protested. Later, one Czech sergeant took down the sign altogether.

Czech Jews who had registered their German nationality in the 1930 census often found themselves in a particularly difficult situation. To the Czech officials, they were Germans. This was regardless of the fact that they were born in Bohemia and survived concentration camps or ghettos. Marianne Zadikowa-Mayova, for example, was affected by such a measure. One administrator wanted to send her to Germany, even though she had returned from Terezin. He said to her, "Miss, as long as you have that German stamp on your ration cards, I won't give you a residence permit. I'm going to give you one now for fourteen days only." She replied, "My mother was born here in 1890, I can bring you a document; I have her birth certificate; her ancestors are from Bohemia on both sides. My father came from Krivoklat and my mother's ancestors came from Prague for generations." He retorted, "That doesn't matter to me, Miss, we are talking about other things today."

Jaroslav Kraus has also had a bitter experience, and even decades after the end of the war, he recalled how he offended some people at an office when he repeatedly heard, "What do the Jews want now?" Zuzana Kalabisova could not forget how she survived her first few nights after returning from Terezin. She was sent to a run-down dormitory. "For four whole years, you dream of returning home, and then you're in a dormitory full of drifters." That was insanely bitter. The administrators wanted one man to change his name from Frantisek Bergman to something more Czech. He replied that if Klement Gottwald (Czechoslovakian president) would change his name, he might consider it.

After all, it was Gottwald and other prominent Communist Party figures who encouraged anti-Jewish sentiment. Vaclav Kopecky, Minister of Propaganda, was particularly prominent in this regard. In 1945, he published a pamphlet entitled "Antisemitism, the Last Weapon of Nazism." A Jewish soldier, Ejsik Weiss, who fought in General Svoboda's Czech Army in the USSR during the war, committed suicide after one of Kopecky's speeches, in which there was mention of Jews inventing or exaggerating their merits in the resistance to support their restitution claims. The Communist Minister Kopecky continued, "*Suppressing anti-Semitism does not mean, for example, helping the Jewish bigwigs à la Petschek, Rothschild, Gutman and so on with their return to the liberated republic so that they can take over their former possessions and continue stealing from our workers. Every citizen of Jewish origin would be subjected to the same rigorous investigation of how he or she behaved nationally in the past and how he or she behaved toward his own Jewish fellows.*"

In an internal document, which was intended only for members of the Communist Party, it was stated, "These bearded Shalamus, these Jewish scums who have only recently joined the domestic or foreign resistance, have no preferential rights over any Czechs."

When Rudolf Slansky, the former General Secretary of the Central Committee of the Communist Party of Czechoslovakia, who was also of Jewish origin, was arrested at the end of 1951 and later sentenced to death in a mock trial, Minister Kopecky declared at a meeting of the Central Committee of the Communist Party of Czechoslovakia, "Hitler persecuted the Jews because they went with us, but now they have a relationship with the Anglo-American imperialism, which supports Israel and speculates on Zionism as a means of internal subversion precisely in the parties of the People's Democratic Establishment and socialism." And Klement Gottwald, in a public speech at the national conference of the Communist Party of the Czechoslovak Republic in 1952, said, "The Zionist organizations and their American principals shamefully exploit the suffering inflicted on the Jews by Hitler and the other fascists. It can be directly said that from the ashes of Auschwitz and Majdanek they capitalized and profited. Similarly, the fight against Zionism has nothing to do with anti-Semitism."

How must Hana have felt when, several years after the Holocaust, she was again confronted with the fact that someone was offended by her Jewish background? She must have been traumatized and deeply dejected. Would the Jewish curse never end?

In contrast, the Fristensky family and the name were made famous, thanks especially to Gustav and his brother Frantisek, my grandfather. Both were successful wrestlers. And both were great Czech patriots. The Fristensky name still resonates in the country today. My father's parents likely thought, "Should they allow a young Jewish woman to spoil the reputation of their great name?"

I am saddened and disappointed that such discrimination happened at all, but when I became more interested in the anti-Jewish sentiment, the early anti-Semitism of my ancestors was very much a reflection of its time. However, nothing is black and white, and the Fristensky family's relationship with Hana soon changed significantly for the better. The main influence of this changed relationship toward acceptance was Hana herself. Despite her horrible Holocaust experience, she possessed an incredible inner strength and stubbornness, complemented by her always smiling and pleasant demeanor.

"She was such a sunshine," recalled my friend Pavel Taussig, who knew my mother very well. She also had a reputation as a superior cook and housekeeper, and she took excellent care of the household. "I think the Fristensky family, and mostly your grandfather, must have been happy in the end that their son Jarek married Hana," Pavel was convinced. "Hanka was a person who could bring people together. I remember when people talked about Hanka Fristenska, it was always in the best light. That was a given! Our children would happily call out when they saw her: 'Auntie, Auntie Hanka has arrived!' And how they jumped into her arms."

Moreover, Hana could completely and absolutely rely on Jarek, who stood behind her even in the most tense moments, and even though it was probably not easy for him either. He felt immense respect for his parents; he was brought up in the spirit of traditional family values and ties. But he would never leave Hana. She really got on well with my father, Jarek. When he passed away decades later, my mother let it be known that she had the kindest husband in the world.

In 1948, as her pregnancy continued, Hana moved back to Zabreh to the home of the Taussig family, who were a tremendous support to her at that time. Jarek joined the army for his obligatory service in September in Dedice near Vyskov, but whenever possible, he took a trip to the Taussigs to see Hana. They had long discussions together about how to resolve the tension with his parents.

Hana came up with the first idea: she told Jarek that she would give up her Jewish faith and join the Czech Brotherhood. Jarek must have known what a difficult step this would be for her, especially in light of the tragic fate met by her parents and other family members. When Hana told him, Jarek hugged her, kissed her, lovingly caressed her arm, then ran his hand down to her already rather large belly, where I was successfully growing. Hana believed that her decision would be appreciated by Jarek's parents, that they would be more welcoming to her and to the expected child after she converted to an acceptable church for them.

As the due date approached, Jarek and Hana also considered names to give their first child. For a boy, Hana had chosen the name Petr in honor of her brother. But for a girl, she was uncertain. She and Jarek were also considering a wedding, but they didn't want to decide the date until they could see how Jarek's parents would react. On their next visit, Jarek told Hana that his father still didn't want to accept her, but he suggested a plan to soften him up. Instead of the name Petr, they could name the boy Frantisek, after the soon-to-be grandfather. Hana agreed. It was another of her sacrifices, but one she never regretted. And so, on November 18, 1948, in the Sanatorium of Corpus Christi in Olomouc, I was born not as Petr but as Frantisek. My grandfather's brother Gustav later wrote about this event in his memoirs, "Frantisek's birth means the salvation of our Fristensky family, concerning the male generation."

Jarek was given a pass from the military for that occasion. He was even allowed to drive to Olomouc in a military car to pick up Hana and her newborn son. A small celebration had already been prepared at the Taussigs' house, to which Hana's former classmate and great friend Svatava had also been invited. And the decision to get married was made. Hana Kleinova and Jaromir Fristensky chose the day of their marriage as Saturday, December 18, 1948, a month after my birth. Their son, born technically out of wedlock, was to become legitimate. The ceremony took place at the Parish Office of the Czech Brotherhood Church in Zabreh. The witnesses were Jarek's brother Dalibor, who came from Prague, and Hana's brother Petr, who came from Hradec Kralove, where he was engaged in military service. Unfortunately, my grandparents, Jarek's father and mother, did not attend. But a major breakthrough was coming.

Not long after the wedding, my parents had me baptized, and my official name on the birth certificate was Frantisek Libor Fristensky. For this ceremony, my grandmother Marie (called Marysa) and my grandfather Frantisek attended. They hugged their daughter-in-law Hana for the first time. The ice finally broke.

But Hana may have possibly harbored some residual familial resentment. Later, when Gustav Fristensky died in the spring of 1957, she did not attend his funeral.

Chapter 24

Bedihost: 1948-1953

A few days after the baptism, we moved to the Fristensky farm in Bedihost No. 7. The main buildings consisted of three main yards surrounded by large farm-outbuildings, living quarters, and an expansive field of vegetables and fruit trees. The agricultural land of about 500 acres behind the farm was leased by my grandfather from the municipality of Bedihost. He mostly cultivated grain, corn, and sugar beets. My father's younger brother Zdenek still lived in Bedihost, while the eldest and youngest brothers (my uncles) lived in Prague at that time.

Life on the farm was similar to life on other farms of that time. My grandfather Frantisek was in the fields, in the stables, or taking care of other business matters from morning until evening. He had many employees, with whom he organized the working day. My grandmother Marie took care of the household, including the kitchen, but she also looked after the small domestic animals such as chickens, pigs, geese, etc. Hana was helpful around the household and learned a great deal from her mother-in-law, as she later acknowledged. My grandmother was pedantic, quite strict, and everything had to be well organized, yet the two women got along very well. However, Hana's primary task was to take care of her son, that is, me. Later, she shared how Marie helped and advised her with everything.

Bedihost is a small village near the town of Prostejov, in the Olomouc region, and it didn't take Hana long to get to know the neighbors and other residents. It is worth mentioning the young Himrova family also had a daughter Hana, who was only a month older than me. My mother probably met Mrs. Himrova in a local shop when the two women were pushing strollers with their children. The families soon became very friendly, as evidenced in several contemporary photographs showing the young mothers during a few country trips together, accompanied by Hana Himrova and me.

My father, Jarek, with his brother Zdenek, took up their great hobby: motorcycle racing. And when he wasn't circling his motorcycle around the racetrack, Jarek was always tweaking and improving the performance of his cherished machine. He used to go to races all over the country, and when he could, he took his wife and son with him. He rebuilt the back of the big Volvo car so that it could accommodate a baby crib. And when he raced, Hana stayed in the depot with the other women, and they took turns looking after me. As my mother told me later, I actually grew up in the middle of the motorcycle racing environment.

At the end of the summer of 1949, while training for a race in Kyjov, Jarek was unfortunately injured. While on the track, the chain of his motorcycle came off. He didn't want to lose any time, so he tried to put the chain back in place. Not a good decision on his part. The chain of his motorcycle cut off the top of three fingers. After this unfortunate event, he concluded his racing career. But he could not give up motorcycles, and for several years he worked as a mechanic for his brother Zdenek, who became a successful Czech motorcycle racer. The nomadic life, from one race to another, was not over for him, Hana, nor me yet.

When I was searching for information about this period of time, I also met Marta Druckerova-Cornell in NYC, who lived with Hana in the same room in Terezin. After the war she worked in Prague in a hotel on Wenceslas Square, as well as for a foreign insurance company. She said that in 1949, the two women met in Prague. "Hanka told me that in Terezin, when her father knew that he had been assigned to a transport, he gave her a piece of paper with two bank numbers and the names of some banks abroad. He confided in her that there was enough money in the accounts for her and her brother Petr, in case they never saw each other again. When I asked her if she still had the paper, she told me that she had lost it long ago. I told her that it didn't matter, that I was sure there were other ways to access the accounts. But Hana told me firmly that she didn't want any German blood money, that her parents would not have approved anyway. And that was the end of the debate on this subject. We continued with our walk in the Stromovka park. I pushed you in a stroller."

Life on the farm in Bedihost went on in a seemingly peaceful rhythm. When I met Mrs. Himrova again after many years, she told me how my mother had confided to her that she was really happy that her new family had finally accepted her as their own. "And Hanka really seemed to radiate contentment at that time. She was always smiling, pleasant, and kind. Jarek, your father, and you really saved her," Mrs. Himrova told me. But Hana was not destined to have many years of a trouble-free and peaceful life.

The post-February 1948 political developments in Czechoslovakia were soon to harshly impact the fate of the Fristensky family. The buzzword of the time was collectivization, with the communist regime taking over all private businesses. The farm in Bedihost, which my grandfather Frantisek had owned since 1939, developed into one of the most successful farm businesses in that region, but was on the verge of becoming a state property. He invested a substantial amount of money in developing and cultivating the farm and providing work opportunities for many town residents. He resisted. It was a fight he couldn't win. In 1952, he was insulted and branded as a "Gulag" (a resistor), and his farm was nationalized; all farming equipment, animals, and private house property were confiscated. The family left the farm with a few suitcases. Their two youngest sons found refuge in other places in the country. In addition, my grandfather and grandmother, Marie, were convicted by the communist court and had to go to prison. My grandparents lost everything in an instant, even their freedom.

Frantisek, Another Wrestler

Frantisek Fristensky is still perceived by many people mainly as the brother of the famous wrestler Gustav. But the truth is that Frantisek was also extremely successful and excellent in this sport. He was born on February 24, 1887, in the village of Kamhajek near Kolin, the youngest of the four Fristensky brothers. Like Gustav, he learned a trade as a butcher. At a young age, he watched his older brother Gustav in training with barbells and witnessed his first wrestling matches. He was very impressed by this and started to train and wrestle as well. Later, the famous wrestling quartet of the Fristensky brothers was formed, including Gustav, Karel, Josef, and Frantisek.

In 1906, Frantisek moved to Brno to join his brother Gustav and continued to improve his wrestling skills. Compared to other professional wrestlers, who usually weighed over two hundred pounds, he weighed only between 175 and 185 pounds. He compensated for this apparent disadvantage with agility, endurance, and excellent technique. Early in his career, he became the champion of Moravia in Brno, a feat he repeated several times. As a wrestler, he traveled throughout half of Europe, but his greatest successes came during his two tours in the United States: 1913/1914 with his brother Gustav and then in 1920/21. However, he was seriously injured during one of his last competitions, which led to the premature end of his promising career. His sporting achievements among professional wrestlers brought him quite a bit of money during this time, which he invested in his first farm in Vendryne near Frydek-Mistek in 1922.

His agricultural and cattle farm was prospering, which allowed him to purchase a distillery and carpentry businesses. In 1926, he sold his deeds in Vendryne and leased, together with Gustav, a larger agricultural and cattle farm in the village of Luzice. Unfortunately, the farm was located in what was then called "Sudetenland," and in 1938, the Fristensky brothers were forced to leave the farm premises, abandoning everything with the exception of personal belongings. As Frantisek was anticipating this event, in the same year he managed to purchase a similar farm in the town of Bedihost.

During the war, he supported the partisan resistance in the Drahanska highland and in the Beskydy Mountains, both financially and by providing much-needed food supplies. After the liberation, he was even rewarded with recognition for his resistance activities by General Ludvik Svoboda, the leader of the Czechoslovak armed forces. But after the communist takeover in 1948, no one paid attention to his support of the resistance. As a gulag, he and his wife ended up in prison in 1953 and lost all his property because Frantisek refused to join the nationalized farming business as required by the communist government. When they were released, he and his wife Marie were rather poor, living in a cottage in the Masecin area near Stechovice, which they were able to borrow (rent-free) from the parents of their daughter-in-law.

In 1960, Frantisek and his wife Marie moved to Roznov to be close to their two sons, relying on their support. My grandfather was constantly looking for work to bring some money into the family, earning extra money as a warehouse worker in the only former brewery. Later, he worked with his son Jaromir, who was in charge of repairing electric motors in the municipal services. His last *major project, however, was the compilation of an extensive history of his and Gustav's wrestling careers, his farming business, and his private life. Later, he gave each of his eight grandchildren a copy of this album. In 1965, he went to visit his son Dalibor at a restaurant and hotel in Kasperske Hory, where he suffered a heart attack. He died on August 17, 1965, and he is buried in the family tomb in Slavkov u Brna.*

The confiscation of the family property and the imprisonment of Jarek's parents must have triggered terrifying memories of the Nazi occupation and Terezin for Hana. She understood this terror firsthand! I am convinced that she must have been shaken by these events. It must have crossed her mind again that this was yet another in a series of punishments for her Jewish origins, even though she had converted to another faith. She had observed communist anti-Semitic attacks at almost every turn. The nagging questions resurfaced: Why? What did I do wrong to whom? Will I never be at peace? Once again, Hana was in a state of fear of what would follow. She knew very well that my grandparents were not the only victims of the class struggle. She knew other families who had "sinned" against the new order, if only because they had some property. Who would follow in their footsteps? Who would be next?

At least there was one piece of encouraging news in a difficult time. Hana became pregnant for the second time. The next addition to the family was expected in early 1953. With her friend Vera Himrova, Hana went for a walk one afternoon among the fields outside the village of Bedihost, both with their small children. They knew each other very well, and they shared their most personal feelings. Vera could tell that Hana's thoughts were elsewhere. "How are you coping at home?" she asked Hana, referring to the arrest of her father-in-law and mother-in-law. Hana knew very well what she was talking about. It was the same case in Himrova's family. "All the people who worked hard every day and improved their own property were punished by the communist regime," said Vera, who hoped Hana might open up.

"Exactly," affirmed Hana. "The same thing happened to my family under the Germans. Everything was taken away from us, then they locked us up like animals and killed most of us. They never told us what we were guilty of," Hana burst out crying.

Vera tried to comfort and encourage Hana. "A man can endure a lot, he even has the strength to do impossible things if he has some reason to do so. And you're about to have your second child, you have a great husband, and a family who loves you. I'm sure everything will be fine again," she assured her.

Hana stopped, turned her head to Vera, wiped her tears, and smiled. "I know, we'll get through everything again, we'll make it. I just don't understand how it's possible. They were Germans, Nazis . . . it was a war time then." She lowered her voice referencing the war, indicating that she wasn't excusing the war time for the atrocities. "But now they are OUR people, even our neighbors, doing very much the same evil. People, who were apparently friends, who knew each other for so long, are treating us now like the Germans did back then. I don't understand, I thought I would never experience anything like this again. Why are they driving us out of our home again?"

After this conversation, Hana and Jarek stayed in Bedihost for a few more weeks near friends. At the end of 1952, they decided to move to Roznov, where Jarek's brother Zdenek and his wife lived. Hana was moving again. It was as if there really was no end to it. But once again the fighter in her awoke, and she demanded of herself that, at 25, she must not let her life be spoiled by events beyond her control.

She was looking forward to having another child.

Chapter 25

Fifteen Years in Roznov
pod Radhostem

My parents and I moved to Roznov in the autumn of 1952. The town is located in the northeast part of Moravia, near Poland and Austria, and it is only a few hours from Auschwitz. Hana didn't know much about the area, just as she didn't know much about her previous post-war homes in Zabreh and Bedihost. She remembered that before the war, she and her parents had several times been in the Beskydy Mountains—specifically in Pustevny and Mount Radhost. This mountain range rises just above the town and defines this picturesque region. Hana recalled the large dominating statue of Radegast, a medieval Slavic god of the sun. This massive statue has a firm place in my childhood memories as well. We also used to visit there with my parents, Hana and Jarek, when we still lived in Bedihost. I think that this mountain town must have conjured pleasant memories for my mother of her parents taking her and Petr there.

The family soon felt very comfortable in Roznov. My father's younger brother Zdenek and his wife were already living there. It didn't take too much time for my parents to be integrated with the daily life of this town. There were several other relatives living in the town and its vicinity, which made the move there even more comfortable. Transitional housing was pre-arranged in a house that belonged to one of Jarek's aunts. It stood in Bezrucova Street. I remember it very well: a living room, which in the evening turned into a bedroom and a small kitchen, that was all. Adjoining the house was a small garden with a wooden shed, where Uncle Zdenek stored his racing motorbike. Across the street was a factory, which was then called MOP (Moravian-Silesian Knitting Factory), where my father got his first job in Roznov.

In January 1953, my brother was born and named after my father—Jaromir (or Jarek). The small apartment became insufficient for a family of four, so in the autumn we moved to a larger two-room apartment on Bozeny Nemcova Street in the Zahumeni housing development. Hana was busy then, and her mother-in-law wasn't around to assist her. There was no time for much reflection on the past. There were two children and a husband to look after as well as running the household. Hana believed that this time her life was again on track, and she was looking forward to the next part of her life. In his free time, Jarek was still helping his brother Zdenek as a motorcycle mechanic as he was racing around the country, but after a year he gave it up to spend more time with his family.

Once Jarek's parents were released from prison, they moved to a small village west of Prague called Masecin. They lived in a large cottage-like chalet with a few acres of gardens and a fruit tree orchard. As children, we spent our summer vacations there.

In Roznov, my mother quickly made friends with women of a similar age and also became a member of the local physical fitness organization, where she and her new friends went to exercise. It really looked like a promising life in a small town at last. At the beginning of 1956, Hana got a job as an accountant in the municipal services of Roznov, and we were also expecting another addition to the family. Despite all of her Terezin resolutions not to have any more children, a third boy was on the way. Why did she change her mind? And three times? Was it a way to cope with the past, when her family was almost entirely exterminated during the Nazi occupation? Or was it the result of a contented and happy life? Parents live on in their children even after their death. The fact that she survived and had children was, in a way, her private tribute to her parents, who did not survive Auschwitz. This must have given her some small comfort despite never mentioning the fate of her parents to us children.

Her third son, Zbynek, was born in September 1956, and Hana and Jarek probably wished for a girl. They let him grow his hair long, which was quite unusual for that time in this country. My parents sent me and my brother to my grandparents' in Masecin for summer vacations. This was especially helpful to them when my youngest brother, Zbynek, was still small, so they could remain at home to look after him. They came to us later when they took a holiday themselves. Often in the summer, my father's brothers would join us there with their families. Sometimes the Fristensky family life in Masecin resembled life on the farm in Bedihost. In my grandfather's heart, after having been an athlete, he was truly a farmer. That was his life desire, fulfillment, and mission. So, in essence, this small farm on the property next to his house was satisfying. The cottage was constantly being improved and adapted by my grandfather for year-round living.

Hana loved to help my grandmother in the tree orchard and vegetable garden and also with the expanding small animals' refuge for chickens, geese, and ducks. Since there was no running water in the house, grandfather dug a well and built water tanks and chicken coops. He was always inventing something for the cottage in order to make it more livable.

I wondered about the mixed feelings my mother might have had as she helped in the garden. She might have viewed her gardening time in Terezin as a small pseudo-freedom despite such harsh conditions. It was there that Hana learned much about tending the vegetables and the fruit trees, cultivating the soil, using garden tools, and mostly using her bare hands. I am convinced that this invaluable experience helped Hana in practical ways on the Bedihost farm and aided in the development of a close relationship with her mother-in-law. Later, when we were living in Roznov, my parents owned a small piece of land where they were planning on building our future house. Grandfather planted fruit trees and vegetable gardens. I often witnessed my mother helping him in this effort. She seemed to enjoy that kind of work. Although Terezin was not an experience she would ever wish for anyone, her resourcefulness learned from those years could now benefit her husband's parents, and it likely made her happy to be able to contribute.

In retrospect, there were many things from my youth that provided hints about my mother's silent past. They make more sense to me in the aftermath of my research.

As a child, I was often sick with bronchitis and spent much time in hospitals with whooping cough. The main treatment then was penicillin, which the nurses injected into my thighs, and I even spent some time in a hospital in Prague. My mother was very worried about me. I struggled with my poor health until the autumn of 1956, when I spent two months in a children's sanatorium that specialized in respiratory issues in Luhacovice Spa. Eventually I recovered, but over the years, I often spent time in hospitals and sanatoriums; I lost my appetite. When everyone at the table had eaten everything, I hadn't even started yet. My mother sat with me at the table until I cleaned the plate. Sometimes it took hours before the plate was empty.

My memory of that time is that no piece of food was ever thrown away in our household. It was not until much later that I realized it was one of the remnants of Hana's Terezin trauma. And one more memory: many times, it happened that when we were all sitting at the table for supper, my mother sometimes didn't put anything on her own plate. She just sat and watched us eat. She anticipated that we children would inevitably not eat the whole meal. And then she would finish whatever we left on the plates, so it was not wasted. Mostly it applied to bony meat such as chicken or pork chops. She collected the bones from our plates and cleaned the remaining pieces of meat, literally to the bone.

My mother was quite strict with us as children, and very particular about hygiene, cleanliness, and neatness. This was undoubtedly another example of Terezin's legacy, where such strict adherence to the daily routine was observed by the room supervisor. My mother also absolutely hated lies. When she found out that we weren't telling the truth, and according to the gravity of the subject, sometimes her favorite wooden spatula had a literal feast on our behinds. We feared that kind of punishment, and it worked!

As the oldest son, my tasks for helping in the household were strictly set by my mother. Some Saturday afternoons were reserved for going to the movies with my friends. And we were really looking forward to it. I knew beforehand that my mother would be the judge of whether I could go or not. I also knew that there were almost every Saturday's housekeeping duties that I was part of, such as cleaning the apartment and doing laundry. My regular job was to scrub the kitchen floor on my knees using a large brush, bucket, and floorcloth, clean the shoes of the whole family, and scrub the doors' thresholds with a steel brush. If my mother wasn't happy with the result, I had to fix it and inevitably missed the movie. There was also a designated time to be back home after playing outside with friends. I had to be home on time. I often sprinted all the way to make sure I wasn't a minute late.

I paid my dues for being the firstborn because my mother was learning how to be a mother with me. I believe that she was guided by her own experiences when she was growing up in Prague before the war. Her childhood ceased when Terezin began. Of course, with my younger brothers, my mother wasn't as strict. But I still remember my childhood very fondly. We actually led a happy family life. My mother loved us. And although she was a bit too stern about some things, she would not fail to make our lives as happy as possible.

During summer vacations, we took various camping trips with my parents around the country. These were really great times. No matter where we were, we always stopped in Masecin at my grandparents' cottage. One time, the family of Uncle Gustav, who lived in Prague, also vacationed with their children there. After a few days, they were leaving to visit the parents of Gustav's wife, Irena, who lived on the other side of Prague. I asked my mother why we didn't have a second pair of grandparents. "They both died a long time ago," she replied. She repeated what she had told me once before, that they had died before the war. Nothing more. No explanation, and she changed the subject. In fact, it was the last time my mother ever referenced her parents in front of me.

My parents and grandparents really enjoyed the small piece of land. Personally, I didn't like to go up there, mostly because my grandfather put me to work. I wanted to spend time with my friends playing sports. It was in a beautiful place overlooking the town with Mount Radhost rising above. When the visibility was clear, even the chapel at the top was visible. My mother liked the view very much. At first, a small cottage was built on the land and next to it a small workshop where my father was repairing small electrical appliances to earn some extra money. He had always dreamed of owning his own auto and electrical repair business.

We spent much free time at the cottage, and in the evenings we had a small campfire going, roasting sausages and enjoying other goodies. Sometimes my parents' friends joined in and after several beers, they were all singing some Czech folk songs. For us children, it was a satisfying time seeing parents as relaxed and untroubled as they could be. The past life experiences of my parents were unknown to me at that time. Much later, I was wondering how difficult that had to have been for them to keep that to themselves. They had no forewarning that another life adversity in the following few years was growing behind the scenes.

In 1962, my grandmother and grandfather moved from Masecin to Roznov. They lived with us for a few months in our small apartment before their new home was to be completed; it had to be built from scratch. My father, his brother Zdenek, and some friends were fixing up a former house near the center square of Roznov that had collapsed some time earlier. Basically, it was an uninhabitable ruin. They rebuilt it into a one-bedroom small apartment for their parents. But there was no running water, no electricity, and no bathroom. That all had to be installed gradually. With no adequate heating, my grandparents spent most of the winter months with us in our apartment. Marta Druckerova-Cornell, a friend of my mother's from the Terezin Ghetto, later told me how Hana remembered living with seven people in a small two-room apartment: "You know, Marta, we were used to living like sardines for three years, so this situation really doesn't bother me at all." Of course, she was referring to Terezin.

It is hard to guess how my mother coped with her memories of the ghetto at that time. Certainly, many of the traumatic experiences came back to her. But she didn't talk about anything; she kept it to herself, hidden from others. In public she was always cheerful, positive, and friendly. I don't remember seeing her sad, sullen, or in a foul mood under normal circumstances. That is why she had many friends among the people of Roznov, or wherever she was, for that matter. She took care of the household and was quite the cook. Her cooking mastery was legendary.

Probably the only family disharmony was over the career of her brother, Petr, who was a professional soldier. Because of this, he also joined the Communist Party. His dream was to work in the Czech Air Force, but without joining the party, he would never be able to accomplish that. He did not have any political ambitions; he just wanted to be successful in his profession, and for that, a "red book" (joining the Party) was a prerequisite in the ideologized progressive army. But for my grandparents, Petr represented a political party that took all of their family property, put them behind bars, and made life miserable until the end of their lives. Naturally, he was not responsible for any of that.

I remember overhearing some very sharp debates about politics among the family members when Petr was visiting, but it was usually my mother who eased the tensions and successfully calmed things down.

Chapter 26

Silence No More

The years passed, and Hana's children grew up and moved from elementary school to high school. It seemed that now she would finally, once again, have some peace in her life. But then came August 21, 1968, the invasion of the "friendly" armies of the Warsaw Pact, led by Soviet tanks. For the longest time, I believed that my father was the one who had decided on emigration from Czechoslovakia. Now, I am convinced that it was my mother who had decided to emigrate—the sooner the better. Enough is enough. Undoubtedly, she replayed in her mind everything she had experienced during the German occupation and the knowledge that more than seventy members of her family and other relatives did not survive the war.

Now the Soviets invaded the country in the same manner as the Nazis did in 1939. "What will happen now?" she must have been thinking. Her emotions must have been crying, "I have three young children, and they are NOT going to take them away from me. NO, this must not happen!" Her resolve for a better future and her conscience told her she did not want to experience anything like that again.

Our immediate family of five headed to Vienna in September 1968 and from there to Switzerland, finding our new home in the town of Chur, the capital and largest city of the canton of Graubunden in the eastern part of the country. It was very unclear at first how my parents had finally chosen Switzerland. It certainly gave her heartache to leave her only family, Petr, behind, but Hana knew that the priority was to keep her sons safe from experiencing the persecution and imprisonment that she had experienced in her childhood.

There were several options; my mother initially dismissed Switzerland, but Germany was definitely not an option for her. My parents also discussed different places in Austria with other emigrants, and the United States was offered, but that seemed too far away. In the end, Switzerland won out. My father had a thriving business in Czechoslovakia but felt he could start again among the Swiss. Once again, my mother was faced with starting her life over to a degree. In the summer of 1971, when I was turning 23, I left the family nest and went to study in another part of the country, but I was always happy to return home, even if it was usually only for a weekend.

In 1978, I emigrated a second time on my own, this time to the United States. Before I left, we occasionally had a few female visitors to our home, whom I had never seen before. Mother seemed very comfortable and joyful with them as if she had known them for a long time. When I asked who they were, the answer was usually, "An acquaintance from Prague." I didn't take any further interest in the women until after my mother's death, when I learned that they were her fellow prisoners from Terezin. They continued to visit my mother in Chur after I left for the US. One of Hana's cellmates, Marta Druckerova-Cornell, who moved to the States after the war, told me, "Whenever I flew from America to Europe, I would write or call your mother, and we would meet. One time she had your daughter Hanka with her. We even met several times in New York. We liked each other very much."

In the late '70s and early '80s, another of her cellmates, Stella Brollova-Repper, flew frequently from the US to Switzerland. "We also met Vera Bendova-Gulikova, who also lived with us in Room 29. First, we met together in her hometown, then we went to see your mother," Stella told me later. "I visited her in Chur about five times. One time there was a pretty little girl with her, a granddaughter. She saw so much of herself in her." Vera emigrated to Switzerland with her husband from the former Czechoslovakia in 1968. I knew Vera in Switzerland because she was a pediatrician for my children. However, I didn't know her past or her connection with my mother. And that was unbelievable, because Vera was one of the girls with whom Hana escaped from the Terezin Ghetto in May 1945.

In 1981, both of my parents visited me in Washington, DC, and I had planned that we would go to Florida to spend time at the beaches near the sea, but my mother had other plans. Instead, she wanted to visit her friends from Prague who had emigrated to the States. We started in New York City and then went out of the city. We visited Marta Druckerova-Cornell and Ella Steinova-Weissberger, as well as Stella Brollova-Repper in Port Washington. But there was no mention of Terezin, and I had no idea at the time where these women knew each other from. They talked about children, about families, and about contemporary life. In hindsight, knowing the circumstances that connected my mother and her friends, I wondered if the silence about Terezin had been pre-arranged. It's probably more likely they needed no spoken guideline; they understandably and innately did not want to recall their shared suffering. Later I asked some of these women if they spoke of Terezin and the camps with each other at any of these visits, and their reply was always a firm "NO!"

Life continued to distance itself from unpleasant times for everyone. In June 1984, I telephoned my parents from the US with happy news: my wife-to-be, Victoria, was pregnant, and we wanted to have a wedding in Chur, Switzerland. My mother was overjoyed, especially when I told her that the baby's name would be Hana for a girl and Petr for a boy. My uncle Petr, living in Prague, promised to come to the wedding too, but he was unable to keep his promise. He wasn't granted a visa from Communist Czechoslovakia until a few days after the ceremony.

There was a period of time when Uncle Petr stayed in Chur for several weeks. It was twelve years after the siblings' last meeting. He had changed his surname to Hron many years earlier, in 1947, to avoid any possible scrutiny and discrimination as a Jew. I often saw my mother and him in the living room together when they were able to spend time together, sitting on the sofa. It seemed to me like they were in a serious discussion. We never wanted to disturb them in their long talks. What was it all about? About Terezin? About their parents and Auschwitz? About happy pre-war moments together? About returning to normal post-war life? We'll never know . . .

Uncle Petr died in Prague, in July 1985, of an incurable disease, a few months after his visit to Switzerland. It must have been another traumatic experience for my mother. She lost the person closest to her. She had felt so alone, except for her bond with Petr, after the suffering of the war, when her parents did not survive. Now, Hana was the last of the immediate Klein family. She really wanted to go to Czechoslovakia for her brother's funeral, but she needed a special permit to enter the country from which she had emigrated 17 years earlier. She even wrote a letter to Communist President Gustav

Husak asking for a three-day permission to attend the funeral, but her request was denied. Just as her parents died in 1944 without her, so too did her brother die forty years later, without her presence.

However, in November 1984, there was an event that shed light on my mother's life once again: her first granddaughter, little Hana, was born. There was no option for a name other than Hana, after my mother. It wasn't long before we were sitting on a plane from the United States to Switzerland with our little Hanicka. This was the beginning of an incredible "parental" relationship between precious Hanka and my parents. It was as if our firstborn daughter had four parents—my parents, in addition to Victoria and me. It was an incredible four years full of love in Switzerland and in the US, where my mother and father often came to visit us. My parents always wished for a daughter. At last, they had one.

At the beginning of 1988, my father Jarek, who "saved" my mother after the war by infusing her with the vigor of life, passed away. My mother must have been in incredible pain, another tragedy in her life, much too soon. But she remained strong and stoic. That's how she was. Only later did she confide in me that if her granddaughter Hana hadn't been sitting next to her at the funeral service, she wouldn't have made it through.

Over the next ten years, the two Hanas developed an incredibly strong bond. It wasn't until after my mother's death, I gradually came to understand what my daughter meant to her. She wasn't just a granddaughter; my mother saw a reflection of herself in her. She saw in her what she could not experience at her age because she was in Terezin Ghetto. When my mother died in 1998, Hana was fourteen. This was the same age when my mother was deported to Terezin. She lived this childhood life with her not only as a grandmother, but as a friend. Her granddaughter Hanka was one of the greatest gifts of her life, she was her personified happiness. All the more because her husband was no longer there.

In 1996, after eight years of living in Switzerland, Victoria and I decided to move back to the United States. It wasn't an easy decision for us at all. Our twins (a son, Misha, and another daughter, Nadia) were born in Switzerland, a few months after my father's death. Many weekends, my mother spent time at her house with all three grandchildren. Her joy was palpable. Yes, it wasn't easy for us to share the news that we would be leaving. How could we break it to her? We thought she would be devastated, trying to convince us to remain in Switzerland. But to my surprise, she took it as if she were already prepared for it. She did not try to persuade us to stay; she never even blamed us for our decision. In retrospect, I realize that this was such a small disappointment compared to everything she had been through in her life.

We settled down in Colorado, and Mother came to visit us a few times. Between those visits, our children were flying to Chur in Switzerland to visit their grandmother during their summer vacation. How the last two years affected her is impossible to guess, but she never showed any negativity. She simply enjoyed her grandchildren when they were with her, cherishing any time she could have with them.

The last time I was with my mother was in Chur on June 21, 1998, to celebrate her 70th birthday. Originally, only our three children, the families of my two brothers, and my uncle Gustav and his wife (my mother's cousin), Irena from Zurich, were there to celebrate that event. Life's obligations persuaded me to remain in Durango, but there was a deep feeling or inner voice urging me that I needed to be there too. It didn't take much more thought when my wife said that I needed to go, even if it would be a brief reunion. I decided that if I went, it would have to be a surprise added to the celebration. Nobody was anticipating that I would show up. I arrived just as the group was getting ready to leave for the restaurant in town for a birthday lunch. I made my mother extremely happy. It was the second time I'd seen tears in her eyes—the first time during our emigration in 1968 in Vienna, and now again thirty years later. Over the course of her life, I only saw brief glimpses of true joy in her eyes, so this was special.

The next day I returned to the States, my children arrived a week later, and my mother went to Roznov where she loved to spend her summer months. Then, a few days later, the phone rang, the precursor to the sad news.

My mother died on July 30, 1998. An incredible life journey of an extraordinary woman, Hana Kleinova-Fristenska, was cut just too short in my view. Death at any age never seems fair, and she should have stayed among us much longer. I reluctantly understand, sometimes, life can be cruel. Yet, at the same time, I suppose, the fact that she survived so much and lived the life she eventually did is what I need to be grateful for.

It is incomprehensible to truly understand the horrors endured by my mother and so many others during the Holocaust. Hana was due to be transported to Auschwitz, but her mother, Marta, went in her place. The principal lines of her nuclear family terminated there, to include her father Rudolf.

However, she lived her life, her trauma laid in her silence. How does one tell the story of survival?

Yet, I stand here with my family as testimony that life somehow finds a way. And the stories must be told.

Afterwords & Appendix

Remembering Our Grandmother

My memories of my Babi [Czech nickname for grandmother] are many. While it has been 22 years since her passing, the void which her absence has created is still very poignant. I spent much of my childhood with Babi: weekends, vacations, and whole summers. There are many memories to speak of and reminisce about, but the things that resonate with me most are the small little interactions. Now that I am an adult, I much more appreciate these daily reminders, and I am thankful that they have remained with me for this long.

The smell of coffee in the morning, and the sound of the coffee maker; I remember waking up after Babi was already awake, seeing her duvet covers pulled back to air out her bed, and then walking to the dining room where she was sitting drinking her cup of coffee. She always greeted me with "Dobry den, kočičko [Good morning, my little kitten]." Now, when I make my coffee in the morning and the aroma wafts through the air, I always hear her voice, and it makes me smile.

I remember the care she took in getting dressed to go to the grocery store, or to meet friends for coffee. Before we went "do města" she would coif her hair just so, put on her freshly pressed blouse and trousers, and put on the most beautiful shade of mauve lipstick. I always admired how well put together she was. When I began going through my early teen years, wanting to be trendy, I remember her being upset with me for having frayed hems at the bottom of my jeans. It was the style then to wear your jeans a bit longer, so naturally the hems would drag along the ground and fray. When I stepped off the airplane to spend the summer with her one year, the first thing she said to me was that I would not be going anywhere with her looking like that. The next day I had a new pair of jeans to wear.

What I didn't understand then, but do now, is the value of taking care of yourself and your possessions. While in my teenage years I began to understand what my Babi had been through as a child, through reading about and studying the Holocaust on my own, she never shared her experiences with me. I tried to inquire about them, but she simply would tell me I was too young to understand. I realize now that she tried to shield me from the unspeakable horrors my Babi had been through, but it took me until adulthood to really learn from the small lessons that she bestowed upon me and to understand their origin. I know now that wasting food was the difference between living and dying for her, and that not taking care of what she had was the difference between having something or having nothing at all.

My Babi didn't spoil me with toys. What she showered upon me was love, sometimes tough, but it was unlimited, nonetheless. She gave me the opportunity to travel, spend time with her and enjoy life much like she would have had Hitler not come to power and destroyed the lives of six million Jews and millions of others left in the wake of the war's destruction. She provided me with the gift of understanding life's precious nuances and moments, and taking care of what I had, and valuing and appreciating what was given to me. I got to see ballets, operas, musicals; travel to the beaches of southern France and Italy; I got to spend time with my family in the Czech Republic and be immersed in the culture; I went on countless walks through the forest behind Babi's house and spent hours just taking to her and listening to stories she told me as we walked amongst the trees. The greatest joy I had was stepping off the train platform and into her arms each weekend when I came to visit; and tears always flowed when I had to get back on the train to go home.

My greatest sorrow, to this day, is losing my Babi. I still cry as if it was yesterday. I cry as I type this now. However, I smile and find comfort despite my tears, when I think of all the days I got to share with her. Memories that guide me still. I always say, "What would Babi say?" I think she would look at me now and say, "Ďelaš to dobře, kočičko [You are doing it well, you little kitten]."

—Hana Fristensky Bruce

In the Jewish faith, when a person has passed on, instead of using the oft-said and well-known wish of "rest in peace," one uses the phrase "may her/his memory be a blessing." My grandmother, whom we lovingly called Babi, was raised in the Jewish faith and would later live through the horribly unspeakable and inhumane events of the Holocaust. This is a letter to my grandmother Hana Fristensky (Kleinova).

Dear Babi,

In an age where email, texting, and social media reign supreme, writing letters is something that is becoming a bit of a lost art in the world of communication. Although it is slowly fading, its memory and practice will never be lost, just like you. I wish I could have talked to you about what life was like before yours changed forever. What was your favorite subject in school? Did you even like school? Where was your favorite place to be alone with your thoughts? Did you like listening to music? I never asked because I didn't know how, and you know how shy and introverted I was.

Instead, I would admire and watch you from a distance. I watched you as we made (what I thought at the time) the long and arduous journey from the market back to your house. I politely say that even at your age, you never once showed the toll that such a journey could take on a person, meanwhile, I thought my legs would fall off from all the walking. Unbeknownst to me, you taught me that strength isn't always your body's ability to do something, but also your mind's. Thank you.

I remember waking up every morning and having to make my bed. It was the last thing a young kid wants to do, but it had to be done because that's how it was living in your house. Our shoes were neatly lined up near the doorway of the house. Our clothes were properly folded and put in their place. If you played with a toy, once you were done with it, it was returned to where it was stored. You would be hard-pressed to find any dirt or dust anywhere. Questioning why these tasks had to be done was futile. The answer was usually because I said so. That answer never satisfied my curious mind, but I knew better than to talk back to you or press the matter. If you could have answered me, then I would imagine you would have said that, "these tasks are learning lessons meant to show you that it is important to take care of our possessions, cleanliness is a virtue, and that a cluttered space is a cluttered mind." To this day, if I feel as though my mind is scattered in many directions, I clean my space and find the clarity I seek in the cleanliness. Thank you.

Most everyone on the planet who has a grandmother who cooks would say that their cooking is the best, but I say in the most shameless, unbiased, factual way that yours tops them all. I know now that food is a powerful conduit to our memory which explains the "grandma's cooking is the best" phenomenon. I wish I had spent more time in the kitchen with you. I was always enamored with the smells emanating from the kitchen. Anytime I would sneak a peek inside your culinary kingdom, I would see the effort and work it took to create the meals I cherished and drooled over. Not only was the food a wonder to behold, but also the act of eating the meal was just as magical. The table was always meticulously set, and everyone was present and seated together. If we had cell phones back then, I know without a doubt you wouldn't have let them anywhere near the table. The focus was on each other and the food that was in front of us. The lessons I learned from the way you treated a meal, whether it was in the preparation, presentation, or how it was eaten, were never disguised.

The love and care that you put into the food was a clear show of the love you had for the people that you shared it with. To me, food was your love language that I understood the most. It's universal and everyone is fluent. You showed me that the time you took to give to others, in whatever way it might be, was time that was never wasted and to be grateful for the moments we can share together. Thank you. I'll always carry you and these lessons with me.

—Michael "Misha" Fristensky

The following was written during my first trip to Israel:

Israel, March 2016

News of my trip was followed by questioning *why are you going there?*

Our visit was guided by a series of interviews with women who had known my Babi, sharing both proximity (women's barracks in Terezin) and experience (Holocaust survivor).

We met Maud Stecklmarerova-Beerova (Terezin survivor, and she knew my Babi) along the muted residential street Shmu'el HaNagid. She spoke softly first *for a long time. I could feel my Babi speaking.*

Meeting these gracious women, well into their 80th and 90th years—surrounded by their books, family portraits, and objects—I couldn't help from wondering with sadness what my Babi would have been like now. I am twenty-eight years old, and have spent more than half of my life without her here. There was so much more to know. My impressions of her are remembered as a silent film—I recall the feelings of the scenes and her movements, expressed by her action. Everything was done and prepared with considered care and intention—how she prepared meals, the combing of her hair, the drawings we, her grandchildren, created, displayed on the wall above the telephone, the ironed linens.

Beit Theresienstadt

The archive at Beit Theresienstadt (Beit Terezin) presented us with a single sheet of Babi's (née Hana Kleinova) compressed Holocaust records. Beside the magenta heading 'fate' reads *liberated.* She was one of 130 surviving children of Terezin out of 15,000. What brought her through to liberation?

She was due to be transported to Auschwitz, but her mother Marta went in her place. The principal lines of her nuclear family terminated there, including her father Rudolf.

Her trauma laid in her silence. How does one tell the story of survival?

—Nadia Fristensky
March 2016

Acknowledgements & Works Consulted

Over fifteen years of researching, compiling, and documenting my mother's story took me on an incredible journey. On this voyage through history, I met many people who were willing to assist me in this "adventure." It was overwhelming. Without their kind contribution, in any form, this testimony could never be heard.

Marie (Mancina) Aschermannova

Pavel Baroch

Doris Beckova-Ostlund

Michele Bergen

Ruth Bondy

Petr Brod

Stella Brollova-Repper

Hana Fristensky Bruce

Tomas Federovic

Jana Renee Friesova

Irena Fristensky

Jarek Fristensky

Victoria M. Fristensky

Beth Green

Ellen Greenebaum

Doris Grozdanovicova

Michael Gruenbaum

Ladislav Gulik

Mirek Hron

Jitka Hronova-Klimova

Maria Klein

Richard Klein

Evelina Landa-Merova

Dagmar Lieblova

Anna Lorencova

Arnost Lustig

Hana Lustigova-Hnatova

Marta Mala

Julius Muller

Fanda Neubaurova-Nassau

Perry Pahlmeyer

John Peel

Paul Salitsky

Maud Steckelmacherova-Beerova

Ilona Steinova-Weinstock

Ela Steinova-Weissberger

Pavel Taussig

Alenka Taussigova

Ruzenka Voglova-Brossler

Vera Weislitzova-Lustigova

Helga Weissova-Hoskova

Richelle White

Works Consulted

Berkley, George E. *Hitler's Gift: The Story of Theresienstadt*. Boston: Branden Books, 2001.

Bondy, Ruth. *"Elder of the Jews": Jakob Edelstein of Theresienstadt*. New York : Grove Press, 1989.

Brenner, Hannelore. *The Girls of Room 28: Friendship, Hope, and Survival in Theresienstadt*. New York: Schocken, 2009.

Epstein, Helen. *Where She Came From: A Daughter's Search for Her Mother's History*. Boston: Plunkett Lake Press, 2019.

Erbenova, Eva, and Marketa Malisova. *Zivot Ely L*. Prague: Franz Kafka Publishing Co., 2013.

Fantlova, Zdenka. *My Lucky Star*. London: SP Books, 2001.

Friesova, Jana Renee. *Fortress of My Youth: Memoir of a Terezin Survivor*. Madison: University of Wisconsin Press, 2022.

Gruenbaum, Michael, and Todd Hasak-Lowy. *Somewhere There Is Still a Sun: A Memoir of the Holocaust*. New York: Simon & Schuster, 2017.

Hayes, Peter. *Why?: Explaining the Holocaust*. New York: W. W. Norton & Company, 2017.

Kraus, Dita. *A Delayed Life: The True Story of the Librarian of Auschwitz*. New York: Random House, 2020.

Lieblova, Dagmar. *Prepsali se, tak jsem tady.* Edited by Marek Lauermann. Marek Lauermann, 2016.

Lustig, Arnost. *Night and Hope.* London: Pickle Partners Publishing, 2017.

Merova, Evelina. *Lebenslauf auf einer Seite.* Berlin: Edition Room 28, 2016.

Noack-Mosse, Eva. *Last Days of Theresienstadt.* Madison: University of Wisconsin Press, 2018.

Oppenhejm, Melanie. *Theresienstadt: Survival in Hell.* London: Menard Press, 2001.

Pollak-Kinsky, Helga, and Otto Pollak. *Mein Theresienstadter Tagebuch 1943-1944: Und die Aufzeichnungen meines Vaters Otto Pollak.* Berlin: Edition Room 28, 2014.

Reiner, Ilse. *Through the Eyes of a Child: "Diary of an Eleven-Year-Old Jewish Girl".* Bloomington, IN: Xlibris US, 2006.

Rubin, Susan Goldman, and Ela Weissberger. *The Cat with the Yellow Star: Coming of Age in Terezin.* New York: Holiday House, 2008.

Ruzickova, Zuzana, and Wendy Holden. *One Hundred Miracles: Music, Auschwitz, Survival and Love.* London: Bloomsbury Publishing, 2020.

Rybar, Ctibor. *Jewish Prague: Guide to the Monuments, Notes on History and Culture.* Prague: TV Spektrum, 1991.

Schiff, Vera. *Hitler's Inferno: Eight Intimate & Personal Histories from the Holocaust.* Toronto: Raj Publishing, 2002.

Schwertfeger, Ruth. *Women of Theresienstadt: Voices from a Concentration Camp.* Oxford: Berg Publishers, 1988.

Sniegon, Tomas. *Vanished History: The Holocaust in Czech and Slovak Historical Culture*. New York: Berghahn Books, 2014.

Snyder, Timothy. *Black Earth: The Holocaust as History and Warning*. New York: Crown, 2015.

Terezin Initiative Institute. *Terezin Studies and Documents*. Prague: Terezin Initiative, 1998-2002.

Weiss, Helga. *Helga's Diary: A Young Girl's Account of Life in a Concentration Camp*. London: Penguin UK, 2013.

The Holocaust and the Family of Hana Kleinova Fristenska

<u>Family Members of Rudolf Ashermann (Hana's maternal grandfather)</u>

	Transport to Terezin	Final Fate
Rudolf Aschermann	---	October 31, 1941 – Lodz †
Zdena Aschermannova-Guthova	February 22, 1942	April 28, 1942 – Zamosc †
Max Guth	February 22, 1942	April 28, 1941 – Zamosc †
Olga Aschermannova-Koralkova	February 22, 1942	April 23, 1942 – Lublin/Piaski †
Hermina Bondy-Aschermannova	---	October 31,1941 – Lodz †
Marta Aschermannova-Kleinova	May 12, 1942	October 16, 1944 – Osvetim †
Karel Aschermann/ Kares	February 4, 1945	Survivor of Terezin
Josef Aschermann	---	October 31, 1941 – Lodz †
Marie Aschermannova-Fuchsova	April 24, 1942	April 28, 1942 – Zamosc †
Jiri Fuchs	April 24, 1942	April 28, 1942 – Zamosc †
Milan Fuchs	April 24, 1942	April 28, 1942 – Zamosc †

Olga Aschermannova-Weissova	June 10, 1942	September 3, 1942 – Ujazdow †
Josef Weiss	June 10, 1942	September 3, 1942 – Ujazdow †
Jiri Weiss	June 10, 1942	September 3, 1942 – Ujazdow †
Milan Weiss	June 10, 1942	September 3, 1942 – Ujazdow †
Otto Aschermann	---	October 31, 1941 – Lodz †

Total: 15 murdered and 1 survivor

Family Members of Simon Klein (Hana's paternal grandfather)

	Transport to Terezin	Final Fate
Simon Klein	June 20, 1942	November 30, 1942 – Terezin †
Ruzena Schwelb-Kleinova	June 20, 1942	Survived Terezin
Moric Klein	September 4, 1942	December 15, 1943 – Osvetim †
Frantisek Klein	September 4, 1942	September 8, 1942 – Maly Trostinec †
Elsa Schultz-Kleinova	September 4, 1942	September 8, 1942 – Maly Trostinec †
Jiri Klein	September 4, 1942	September 8, 1942 – Maly Trostinec †
Ivan Klein	September 4, 1942	September 8, 1942 – Maly Trostinec †
Anna Kleinova	January 30, 1942	Survived Osvetim
Karel Klein	January 30, 1942	May 18, 1944 – Osvetim †
Frantisek Klein	December 5, 1942	September 6, 1943 – Osvetim †
Milan Klein	December 5, 1942	September 6, 1943 – Osvetim †
Bedrich Klein	August 10, 1942	September 1, 1942 – Raasiku †

Hermina Kleinova-Zenker	November 26, 1942	January 20, 1943 – Osvetim †
Rudolf Zenker	November 26, 1942	January 20, 1943 – Osvetim †
Marta Zenker-Blochova	June 20, 1942	Survived Osvetim
Karel Bloch	June 20, 1942	October 19, 1944 – Osvetim, Dachau †
Vladimir Zenker	November 26, 1942	January 20, 1943 – Osvetim †
Oto Zenker	November 26, 1942	January 20, 1943 – Osvetim †
Richard Klein	November 26, 1942	January 20, 1943 – Osvetim †
Frantiska Ehrmann-Kleinova	November 26, 1942	January 20, 1943 – Osvetim †
Artur Klein	May 12, 1942	October 12, 1944 – Osvetim †
Irma Bony-Kleinova	May 12, 1942	October 12, 1944 – Osvetim †
Ota Klein	December 4, 1941	Survived Osvetim
Rudolf Klein	May 12, 1942	October 16, 1944 – Osvetim †
Hana Kleinova-Fristenska	May 12, 1942	Survived Terezin
Petr Klein-Hron	May 12, 1942	Survived Osvetim a Meuselwitz
Anna Kleinova-Dusnerova	May 7, 1942	May 9, 1942 – Sobibor †
Vilem Dusner	May 7, 1942	May 9, 1942 – Sobibor, Majdanek †

Ivan Dusner	May 7, 1942	May 9, 1942 – Sobibor †
Karel Klein	May 12, 1942	May 17, 1942 – Majdanek †
Josefa Szuranova-Kleinova	May 12, 1942	May 17, 1942 – Majdanek
Rudolf Klein	August 10, 1942	February 1, 1943 – Osvetim †
Emil Klein	December 4, 1941	September 28, 1944 – Osvetim †
Marie Steinerova-Kleinova	---	June 10, 1942 – Ujazdov †
Eva Kleinova	---	June 10, 1942 – Ujazdov †
Frantisek Klein	February 4, 1945	Survived Terezin
Ruth Frunbergova-Kleinova	December 14, 1941	Survived Osvetim and Bergen-Belsen

*Total: **29 murdered and 8 survivors***

Transports from Terezin Ghetto

Designation	Day of Departure	Number of Prisoners	Destination	Number of Survivors
O	Jan 9, 1942	1,000	Riga	105
P	Jan 15, 1942	1,000	Riga	16
Aa	Mar 11, 1942	1,001	Izbica	7
Ab	Mar 17, 1942	1,000	Izbica	3
Ag	Apr 1, 1942	1,000	Piaski	5
Ap	Apr 18, 1942	1,000	Rejowiec, Sobibor	3
Al	Apr 23, 1942	1,000	Lublin	1
An	Apr 25, 1942	1,000	Warsaw	9
Aq	Apr 27, 1942	1,000	Lublin, Izbica	1
Ar	Apr 28, 1942	1,000	Zamosc	1
As	Apr 30, 1942	1,000	Zamosc	5
Ax	May 9, 1942	1,000	Ossowa	0
Ay	May 17, 1942	1,000	Lublin	0
Az	May 25, 1942	1,000	Lublin	1
AAk	Jun 12, 1942	1,000	Trawniki	0
AAi	Jun 13, 1942	1,000	Unknown	0
AAx	Jun 14, 1942	1,000	Maly Trostinec	2

AAy	Jun 28, 1942	1,000	Baranovici	0
AAz	Aug 4, 1942	1,000	Maly Trostinec	2
Bb	Aug 20, 1942	1,000	Riga	0
Bc	Aug 25, 1942	1,000	Maly Trostinec	1
Be	Sep 1, 1942	1,000	Raasiku	45
Be	Sep 8, 1942	1,000	Maly Trostinec	4
Bo	Sep 19, 1942	2,000	Treblinka	0
Bp	Sep 21, 1942	2020	Treblinka	0
Bn	Sep 22, 1942	1,000	Maly Trostinec	1
Bq	Sep 23, 1942	1,980	Treblinka	0
Br	Sep 26, 1942	2,004	Treblinka	0
Bs	Sep 29, 1942	2,000	Treblinka	0
Bt	Oct 5, 1942	1,000	Treblinka	0
Bu	Oct 8, 1942	1,000	Treblinka	2
Bv	Oct 15, 1942	1,998	Treblinka	0
Bw	Oct 19, 1942	1,984	Treblinka	0
Bx	Oct 22, 1942	2,018	Treblinka	0
By	Oct 26, 1942	1,866	Auschwitz	28
Cq	Jan 20, 1943	2,000	Auschwitz	2

Cr	Jan 23, 1943	2,000	Auschwitz	3
Cs	Jan 26, 1943	1,000	Auschwitz	39
Ct	Jan 29, 1943	1,000	Auschwitz	23
Cu	Feb 1, 1943	1,001	Auschwitz	29
Dl	Sep 6, 1943	2,479	Auschwitz	10
Dn (children)	Oct 5, 1943	1,196	Auschwitz	0
Dn/a	Oct 5, 1943	53	Auschwitz	0
Dr	Dec 15, 1943	2,504	Auschwitz	279
Ds	Dec 18, 1943	2,503	Auschwitz	449
Dx	Mar 20, 1944	45	Auschwitz	0
Dz	May 15, 1944	2,503	Auschwitz	120
Ea	May 16, 1944	2,500	Auschwitz	8
Rum	May 17, 1944	5	Bergen-Belsen	0
Eb	May 18, 1944	2,500	Auschwitz	273
Eh	Jul 1, 1944	10	Auschwitz	0
Eg	Jul 4, 1944	15	Bergen-Belsen	0
Ej	Sep 27, 1944	20	Bergen-Belsen	0
Ek	Sep 28, 1944	2,499	Auschwitz	382
El	Sep 29, 1944	1,500	Auschwitz	79

Em	Oct 1, 1944	1,500	Auschwitz	306
En	Oct 4, 1944	1,500	Auschwitz	128
Eo	Oct 6, 1944	1,550	Auschwitz	78
Ep	Oct 9, 1944	1,600	Auschwitz	23
Eq	Oct 12,1944	1,500	Auschwitz	78
Er	Oct 16, 1944	1,500	Auschwitz	117
Es	Oct 19, 1944	1,500	Auschwitz	53
Et	Oct 23, 1944	1,715	Auschwitz	186
Ev	Oct 28, 1944	2,038	Auschwitz	144

Sources: *Holocaust.cz*; *Karny*, The Final Solution

Quotes from the Diaries of Terezin Ghetto Survivors

"The block houses with their filth, where one sick person lies infected with dysentery on top of another, where corpses and those who are almost corpses lie all day pressed side by side, where mattresses decompose with dampness and cannot be replaced, because hordes of worms are found underneath."

"The rooms are full of people. Excrements all over, lack of eating utensils, the dead lie among the living all day."

"We see people begging for scraps of bread throughout the barracks, begging for crumbs of food at the kitchens and dispensaries, begging for potato peelings to be kept for them, and gasping for those pittances with their emaciated hands."

"One mother, who has measles, lies with her children who are also sick. Women who have gone to the hospital with their children return without finding their place, which, by then, was occupied by others. A 14-year-old boy has died."

"The old people were dropping like flies because after standing for fourteen hours they couldn't stand it anymore."

"The year 1942 is drawing to a close and with its last day the question floods our hearts and minds: 'Will the new year 1943 bring an end to the present war?' The ghetto awaits the new year with the utmost hopes. Yet people live in attics and dark corners, on the ground, and in cellars. We enter the new year 1943 with the singing of our Czech anthem 'Where is My Home?'"

"The present state of affairs, where bed bugs have invaded our quarters and forced the occupants to sleep in yards, corridors, etc., is untenable."

"The misery of these old Jewish Germans is unimaginable. They go from room to room all day long, begging for a piece of bread."

"The deliveries of parcels have been stopped; they say only two thousand will be allowed per month, as many as there have been so far per day. Those who wished could fill out a form on which it was stated that the person named was asking for a stamp for the person, who will send the parcel. It's a double-edged sword. Shall we name someone in Prague? Wouldn't that cause him trouble, because he's connected with the Jews?"

"The day ended with Daddy opening the first and the last can of sardines."

"Old people do not have neither room nor peace to die. They won't be able to use the toilets because the drainpipe is blocked."

"For more than fourteen days now the whole tailoring department has been relentlessly working to repair thousands and thousands of parts of the uniforms of the German soldiers. After the repairs have been made, these uniforms are being made ready for winter with a white coating on one side of the garments."

"The bread has been totally stale lately. One gets used to everything: also to repulsive and terrible things."

"Yesterday Magda had a surprise for us. Prof. Eisinger came to visit us and sang three songs for us. I was thrilled."

"A transport from Pilsen arrived. Lots of friends. The elderly (one woman in her nineties), the sick and only a few able to work came."

"New productions are being set up for the war effort. We are forced to help them."

"There is one child left out in the list of those to be reclaimed from the transport . . . he died. The old men and women are living in the barracks with no toilets and no washrooms."

"People are begging you for soup. Soup that's just warm water. A man who gets a parcel, doesn't get a soup."

"Yesterday, I went to see an opera. Even though it's sung accompanied only with piano, no costumes and no sets, the impression at the Prague's National Theatre couldn't have been better."

"Yesterday the orphans from Frankfurt arrived. We almost didn't know where to put them."

"People are slowly freezing to death in the barracks, especially in the attics, where there is no heating at all. At ten degrees below zero, people have already been found frozen, one person lying on top of another."

"When are we going home? That is the motto of Terezin. How victory will look like."

"There are daily concerts, lectures, theatre, even a show. And at the same time, German Jews are starving to death in the block houses."

"Nine people arrested for smuggling letters were hanged. The sentence had to be carried out by Jews. Despair everywhere."

"A transport will go from here to Poland. Will we be on it? It's terrible. We thought that at least before that we would be safe here, now we are in the same situation as we were in Prague."

"Inside the 'Hunting Barracks,' people were hiding under and behind beds, under toilet boards, whole families, who just didn't go to the assembly place when they were called up, and seemingly were successful."

Source: Museum of the Terezin Ghetto, The Terezin Memorial

The Secret of the Terezin Attic

A few years ago, when the Terezin guide Lukas Lev moved from one house to another in the former ghetto, it was very hot, so his new landlord told him to turn on the boiler above the staircase to the attic so that he could rinse himself under warm water. Lukas Lev couldn't find it, but what he discovered in the attic took his breath away: on the walls were writings and drawings of former Terezin prisoners. He saw a picture of the Prague Castle above the Charles Bridge and also a short poem about the bedbugs that plagued the exhausted and sick Jewish inhabitants. The author was probably a Dutch woman: "O bedbug, O bedbug, O little bedbug – O you ugly beast that dances all night over me. My limbs are twitching from the very scratching, I can feel you crawling up and down – from my head to my toes." Or next to the date February 13, 1944, there was a scribble scratched in the wall: "Jirka is an asshole."

"That room has been closed probably since World War II," Lev says. Then he heard from a colleague from the Terezin Initiative, which, among other things, documents and commemorates the victims of the "Final Solution to the Jewish Question" in the Czech lands. She had discovered a document from the time, according to which four specific boys also passed through this attic. Because they had inadequately closed the window's shades at night as instructed by the ghetto's Nazi administration, they were forbidden to turn on the lights for eight days. "I began to search for their fate," says Lukas Lev.

He found out that three of them were from Prague and one from the village of Bavorov in South Bohemia. In fact, on one wall in the attic, a two-line inscription can still be read: "My dear Bavorov, a village under Sumava Forest." Only two of them lived to see the liberation, although both were assigned to the transport to Auschwitz. From there they were sent to other camps, one of them returned to Terezin before the end of the war. After the liberation, both of them went to the Americas—one to the United States, the other to Colombia. "I am still in contact with the daughter of one of them, she lives in Bogota," Lev says.

After discovering inscriptions and drawings on the walls, he set about further exploring the former ghetto. "I went house to house and asked the tenants if they would let me into the attic. And they usually did," he recalls. In one house, for example, he discovered beautifully painted palm trees with a small tiger. He also discovered an original bakery from the ghetto era. And in one courtyard, he found a shed with the Ohre River along the stairs and a Terezin church on the second floor with the inscription 1944.

But the shed no longer exists, the owners demolished it. Other monuments to the Terezin ghetto also ended in a similar way. For example, transport tickets or period crockery. "One lady told me, for example, that during the reconstruction of her house she had to order a container of how much there was. She said some suitcases and papers with clipboards. They ended up in a landfill somewhere," says Lukas Lev. This cannot happen in the case of the attic that Lukas Lev discovered a few years ago. The Terezin guide has built a small museum there and takes visitors on a tour of the former ghetto.

There are other positive examples. For example, in the autumn of 2019, during the reconstruction of the house, many documents from the ghetto era were discovered in the attic that could not be accessed earlier, including a straw mattress, a suitcase, clothes pegs, and beer bottles from the local brewery. "We also found numbers that were originally sewn on various pieces of luggage, or long strips of cloth marked with a permanent ink that were used to mark the items when they went to the laundry. This find is truly unique," says Michaela Dostalova, head of the documentation department at the Terezin Memorial. She described the surviving list of toilet services in one of the Terezin barracks as a very interesting rarity.

Lukas knows the former Terezin Ghetto very well, and sometimes, he is able to take his visitors to places that are not on the regular ghetto tour agenda. After thorough research, he helped me to locate the exact spot where my mother, starring in the 1944 Nazi propaganda movie, was working in the garden. That was a very emotional discovery for me.

Reviews from Readers of the Czech Version

A review of **My Mom from Terezin: The Secret Story of a Jewish Woman Discovered Years Later by Her Son.** *Written by Frank Fristensky. 12/2021.*

"The fate of Frank's mother, Hana Kleinova, was at one time shrouded in mystery and, above all, silence. So, all three of her sons knew nothing about the fact that their mother had spent three long and cruel years in the concentration camp at Terezin Ghetto (1942-1945).

In 352 pages the life of 14-year-old Hana is very sensitively described, who after the occupation was forced with her parents and brother to abruptly alter her young and happy life to a life where all freedom lost its meaning and only terror, fear and the will to survive remained.

The book is also remarkable for the fact that in each chapter there are historical stops that supplement the facts according to real history. And when you get to the transports from Terezin, where you see in a table how many prisoners survived.

19 September 1942 – 2,000 prisoners – Treblinka – 0 survivors

5 October 1943 – 1,196 children – Auschwitz – 0 survivors

18 May 1944 – 2,500 prisoners – Auschwitz – 449 survivors

The search of Frank Fristensky for his mother's unspoken past lasted nearly twenty years. It was worth it.

This powerful story of one woman, one mother, and her son trying to fill an unknown place in her life was written after the death of the main character.

Like me when I read it, Frank's search for his mother's fate made him realize the power of his family's genes and that the white spaces in the lives of loved ones can be filled and passed on through time and space.

That good deed is undoubtedly the book *My Mom from Terezin*."

—Libuse Rousova (Roznov), January 2022

"Frank Fristensky wrote his book *My Mother from Terezin* (My Mother from the Terezin Ghetto) about his mother's life before he was born in 1948, because she never talked about this stage of her life. He found out that 14-year-old Hana Kleinova was deported with her parents and brother to Terezin in 1942, where, thanks to her mother, who rescued her from the transport to the East, she remained in the Terezin Ghetto until the end of the war. Unfortunately, her parents and grandparents were not so lucky. The author proclaims a search through his mother's past with scenes from her life and related historical inserts and explanations. I would recommend the book to readers who are not too familiar with the Holocaust and political history before and after the war."

—Cori, May 13, 2022

"Actually, I was expecting something a little different. Nevertheless, I liked the book very much for its unconventionality. We encounter the theme of war either in a story or in non-fiction, but to combine both is a bit unconventional, and yet presented in a very sensitive way . . . I know from my own experience how much work goes into composing such a text and, therefore, I bow down at the author's effort and his "enthusiasm" to finish everything while there are still witnesses of Hanka's years lived in Terezin."

—Gabra03, February 13, 2022

"I read your book with great interest. It is a great read and I admire you, what all and in what way you have learned what you knew nothing about. I know almost all the girls you mention. I've met Ella Weisberger many times. I even stayed at her house in Tapan. I'm sorry I don't remember your mother. We both lived in L410 in the same corridor, I in room 24, she in room 29. I know the film. May the book find many readers and be a success."

—Helga Hoskova-Weissova, survivor of the Theresienstadt ghetto, Auschwitz, Freiberg, and Mauthausen

"This fascinating book has been written in a rather unconventional form. It is mainly non-fiction, but you will also find elements of a novel. It tells about the connection of Holocaust with the well-known Czech Fristensky family. It tells about the cruelties of the Terezin Ghetto, but also about hope and love."

—LukBook, February 25, 2022

"I'm just reading a book you wrote about your mother. It is very engaging and uniquely written. I read a lot of literature on the Holocaust and your book is one that has interested me very much for a long time."

—Michaela Novakova, January 18, 2022

"I am glad to be able to write the first comment on this interesting book. But my expectations were a bit different. I thought it was going to be more focused on Hana's life. It was more about the facts, but of course I understand that even what is in the book must have been a real job to find out. To organize a meeting with the survivors . . . and to go through the time lines. I also very much appreciate the links to other books and materials about the Holocaust. I believe that thanks to this, the author had the opportunity to learn his mother's secret and understood a lot of things in retrospect. It is obvious that the author devoted a lot of time to publish the book."

—Zdenule27, December 13, 2021

Interview with the Author

From an interview with Frank Fristensky by Andrea Zunova (*Pravo* newspaper), November 12, 2021.

When he [Frank Fristensky] asked his mother about his grandfather, grandmother and other relatives on her side, she always told him that they had died before the war. And she didn't say anything more about them. As a child, he didn't worry about it. He graduated and started his own business after emigrating to America. His friends teased him that he should write a book about his life. And so he started looking into his ancestors.

It was clear from Daddy's side. It was Gustav Fristensky, the famous wrestler and his brothers. Mom's side was just a brother. But Frank Fristensky didn't give in. He found out that his mother, Hana Klein, had spent three years in the Terezin ghetto. Only she and her brother Petr survived the Second World War and the Holocaust. Neither had ever spoken about their trauma.

Frank wrote a book about his mother and her difficult life story, *My Mom from Terezin* [Czech title]. It was given literary form by the publicist Pavel Baroch. The book will be published by the publishing house Zed' with the support of the Holocaust Victims Foundation. It will be published on 1 December, the 80th anniversary of the founding of the Terezin ghetto.

Your mother came to Terezin at the age of 14 and spent three years there. Didn't you know that as a child?
My mother didn't talk about it at all. She never talked about Judaism, about what happened to her parents, her family, herself, her friends. It was a huge trauma for her. She lived with it for the rest of her life, keeping this secret to herself. She was often sad.

Her brother Petr, who was transported from Terezin to Auschwitz, then to another camp and then further west to Germany, survived. The train they were on was bombed. A lot of people died, but many also escaped. Among them was Peter. They were the only ones who survived from the whole family.

Now that I've got it all mapped out, I understand that everything she went through must have been a huge trauma for my mother, and she couldn't talk about it.

How do you explain that?

I think there are two groups of people. When I came to America in 1976, I lived for a while with Arnost Lustig's family. He talked about the Holocaust and his children Eva and Pepi knew exactly what had happened, they knew about their family. That was not the case with my mother.

So I call one group the Arnost group. These are people who talk about what they lived through because they think that the next generation needs to know about it. My mother didn't think that way. And so she's in the other group of people who didn't talk about it.

What made you want to find out about your mother's story?

When I started telling my life story to friends, especially in America, they said I had to write it down and that it could be made into a movie. I started with stories of my parents and realized that I could write very little about my mom. I only knew about my mom's life from the time I was born going forward. But what was before that?

When I was little and asked why I didn't have second grandparents, she said they died before the war. And aunts and uncles? They all died before the war. She never said more.

It wasn't until Arnost Lustig told me that my mother was Jewish. I didn't know what that meant, but I knew that when I was little, my parents and I used to go to Zabreh in Moravia. My parents were friends with the Taussigs, and Paul Taussig and I refer to ourselves as cousins.

It wasn't until I was much older that I found out that Paul's parents took care of my mother when she returned from Terezin. Rudolf Taussig, Pavel's dad, was already dead, but Alenka, his mom, knew a lot. So she told me. That's where I first learned about Terezin and that my mother's whole family had gone up the chimney, so to speak.

What was your mother's family like?
Close-knit, did a lot of things together. I think the most important thing to my mom was her dad. There's a lot of pictures of her with him, and one of her writing: There's my dear Daddy. When she and Peter returned to Prague after the war, they didn't know what had happened to the family and hoped they would come back. They waited there several months. In vain.

Who else did you talk to besides Mrs. Taussig about your mother?
I interviewed several ladies who knew my mother, who were with her in Terezin. They were in their nineties and still called themselves girls. That was very nice. When they told me their stories, it was like I was talking with my mother. Some of them had lived in the same quarters with her, they had the same work in agriculture, in the gardens of Terezin.

Their daily routine was more or less the same. But they lived in permanent fear. They didn't know what would happen tomorrow. Every day there was the threat of transport, they suffered from hunger, illness and cold. When you fight for your life every day for three years, it must mark you.

Your mother was in Terezin till the end of the war?
Yes, she was lucky. But she was selected for transport to Auschwitz. But she was recalled. That was sometimes successful. But unfortunately, someone else was put in her place. The totals must end up right.

At first, the Germans transported whole families from Terezin. And Rudolf Klein, my mother's father, once or twice was able to successfully recall his family. After that, whole families were no longer kept together for transport, and finally, Mom was supposed to go with her dad. But her mother put herself on the transport list instead.

That saved [my mother's] life. [My grandmother] asked Hilda Taussig Sladka, with whom she worked in one of the kitchens in Terezin, that if they didn't come back, if she would take care of her daughter.

Your mother must have been a very strong woman because she thought she would protect you by not telling you and your brothers anything about her trauma.
Yes, I agree. The people I talked to confirmed it. They wanted to protect their children. They were protecting their children from what's called second-generation syndrome. But it also has to do with the fact that I've rarely seen my mother cheerful.

Your life is colorful. You and your parents first emigrated to Switzerland, then you went to America, where you started a sports business.
With my sporting background on my dad's side, I guess I didn't really have a choice. But I've always enjoyed sports.

Did you do well?
When I first came to America, I wasn't even 30 years old and I was doing what I had dreamed of doing. I was teaching gym classes, coaching women's college volleyball. I figured it couldn't get any better. My grandfather Frantisek, the youngest brother of Gustav Fristensky, had been in America twice, on a wrestling competition tour in 1913-14 and 1920-21. He did very well there, and made good money.

When I was about fifteen, in Masecin (small village outside of Prague), where he and my grandmother lived at that time, he told me: If you want to make it in life, you have to go to America. And when I was working in America in 1978, I said with eyes uplifted to heaven, "Grandpa, if you can hear me, I made it!" America was a dream come true for me.

Now you and your wife, who is American, live in the Czech Republic. But your children are in America. Why did you decide that?
I always felt I was Czech. Let me tell you a nice story. One day Pepi Lustig took me and my brother to Jiri Voskovec (well-known Czech

comedian and actor) in California. He told us about his grandmother, who took a train trip to Russia in the early 1900s. She was sitting in the compartment with this big gentleman who was sleeping.

When the train stopped somewhere, it was late in the evening, and the gentleman got up and said, "Madam, are you hungry? I'm going to buy something." She said no, and he brought back a big steak for himself. Then he introduced himself as Gustav Fristensky and said he was going to a wrestling tournament in Russia.

When his grandmother told Voskovec this story later, he told her, "Grandma, you're so stupid, why didn't you engage in conversation more, I could have been the famous Fristensky, not a stupid Voskovec."

And as he told us this story, I realized that even after so many years of living elsewhere, he spoke such beautiful Czech! His Czech was excellent.

You speak great Czech too.

I was so excited that I said to myself that I mustn't forget my Czech. When we went to Switzerland, my youngest brother was 10 years old. There they spoke German at school and Swiss on the street. It made a bit of a goulash. When my little brother was talking to my mother one day and she was telling him, "That's a prostitution of speech. You're mixing Czech with German, either you speak German to me or you speak Czech. But don't mix the two together!"

When my first daughter was born in 1984, my parents didn't speak any English, and I thought, I'm not going to speak German to my daughter in America. She was their first granddaughter. After she was born, I welcomed her in Czech. I now have three adult children, and they all speak Czech. They even get upset sometimes now when I happen to speak English to them.

About the Author

Frank Fristensky was born in November 1948 in Olomouc (former Czechoslovakia), the first son of Hana Kleinova and Jaromir Fristensky. He is the grandson of Frantisek Fristensky, a well-known professional Greco-Roman wrestler, later a landowner, and brother of the more famous Gustav Fristensky, also a professional wrestler. Frank graduated from the Technical College in Valasske Mezirici in 1968. Shortly thereafter, he moved to Prague, where he worked for the National Military Construction Company as a technician. Following the Soviet-led invasion of Czechoslovakia in August of 1968, he emigrated in September of that year with his parents and two young brothers to Switzerland, where he was the first student of the Eastern Bloc countries to graduate from the National Sports Institute.

In 1978, Frank moved to the USA, first to Washington, DC, where he worked as a physical education instructor and head volleyball coach at American University. In 1982, he continued with his coaching career in Ypsilanti, Michigan, at Eastern Michigan University. He and his growing family moved to Durango, Colorado, in 1996, where he taught physical education at Fort Lewis College and later operated fitness centers specializing in personal training. Since 2018, Frank and his wife Victoria have lived in the Czech Republic. Their three children, Hana, Misha, and Nadia, live in the USA. After his mother's death in 1998, realizing her secret past, Frank's mission became to write her life story.

About the Co-Author

Pavel Baroch was born in February 1968 in Karlovy Vary (in then Czechoslovakia). He graduated in journalism from Charles University in Prague. Since 1990, he has worked as a journalist for various Czech daily and weekly publications, including time with Czech television. Baroch was awarded several prestigious Czech journalistic awards. Additionally, he has authored and published two books *Mengeleho Dvojce A-782* (*Mengele's Double A-782*) and *10,000 Kroku* (*10,000 Steps*). He contributed to the historical context for Fristensky's original book, *My Mother from Terezin*, which has been translated into English for *Silence Finally Speaks*. He is married, has a daughter and a son, and they live in Prague.

About the Editor

Richelle White has been a freelance writer and editor since 2005, with degrees in Written Communications, Visual Communications, and Technical Writing. She has known the author, Frank Fristensky, since 1983, when he was her college volleyball coach at Eastern Michigan University. White considers her editing work on the English translation of *Silence Finally Speaks* among the most rewarding of her projects. She resides in Maryland when she is not traveling.

About the Publisher

The Sager Group was founded in 1984. In 2012 it was chartered as a multimedia content brand, with the intent of empowering those who create art—an umbrella beneath which makers can pursue, and profit from, their craft directly, without gatekeepers. TSG publishes books; ministers to artists and provides modest grants; and produces documentary, feature, and commercial films. By harnessing the means of production, The Sager Group helps artists help themselves. For more information, please see TheSagerGroup.net.

More Books from The Sager Group

The Swamp: Deceit and Corruption in the CIA
An Elizabeth Petrov Thriller (Book 1)
by Jeff Grant

Chains of Nobility: Brotherhood of the Mamluks (Books 1-3)
by Brad Graft

Meeting Mozart: A Novel Drawn from the Secret Diaries of Lorenzo Da Ponte
by Howard Jay Smith

Death Came Swiftly: A Novel About the Tay Bridge Disaster of 1879
by Bill Abrams

A Boy and His Dog in Hell: And Other Stories
by Mike Sager

Eat Wheaties: A Novel
by Michael Kun

Goodbye, Sweetberry Park: A Novel
by Josh Green

Lifeboat No. 8: Surviving the Titanic
by Elizabeth Kaye

Hunting Marlon Brando: A True Story
by Mike Sager

Sing Sing Follies (A Maximum-Security Comedy): And Other True Stories
by John H. Richardson

Who She Was: My Search for My Mother's Life
By Samuel G. Freedman

See our entire library at TheSagerGroup.ne

Artifex Te Adiuva